The Secret Diary of

A LORD GNOME

Aged 73¾

EDITED BY IAN HISLOP

PRIVATE EYE/ANDRE DEUTSCH

Published in Great Britain by Private Eye Productions Ltd.
6 Carlisle Street, London W1.,
In association with André Deutsch Ltd.,
105 Great Russell Street, London WC1.
© 1985 Pressdram Ltd.

Reprinted 1985 (Three Times)

Typeset by Columns of Reading
Printed in England by
The Bath Press, Bath, Avon.

Designed by Roger Lightfoot

THE BEST OF
PRIVATE EYE
1982–1985

THEY
DIED
TO SAVE
HER FACE

THE
FALKLANDS
1982

NEW WAR MEMORIAL

Radio 3

**121.5kHz/247m
VHF:90-92.5**
Frequency details: page 37

Time: GTS 7.0 8.0 9.0 am

Andrew Lloyd George: 9.05

7.00 News Weather
7.05
Morning Concert
Galtieri: Overture in F
Buenos Aires Radio Symphony
Orchestra, conducted by Sir Rex
Hunt.
San Carlos: Piano Concerto No 5
Lami Dozo (guitar) Petit
Orchestre de Limoges. Conductor:
Pym Hoo Hee.
Woodward: On Goose Green (song
cycle) Max Hastings (tenor),
Nicanor Costa Mendez (piano).

8.00 News & Weather

8.05
Aubade
Gueritz: Symphony No 8 (The
Bavarian)
Orchestre des Harpes, conductor
Sir Brian Marhanahan.
Menendez: Orchestral Suite "Las
Malvinas" Camerata Academica
Neasdensis. Conductor: Sir
Alexander Haig.

Sibelius: Tone Poem Falklandia
Daily Telegraph Symphony
Orchestra. Conductor: Sir William
Deedes

9.00 News & Weather

9.05
Composer of the Week
Perez de Cuellar
Guitar Concerto
Andrew Lloyd-George (guitar)
Evita Symphony Orchestra.
Conductor: Sir Ian McDonald
Ballet Suite: "The Flight of the
Pucara" Solisti di Montanas Dollis
Conductor: Sir Hugo Dennisman.

9.40
Organ Recital
John Nott (organ)
Taskfuss: Prelude in A.
Junta: Exocet (1974)
Nott: Resume in B flat
*(Broadcast live from the Church
of the Blessed Margaret, Grantham,*

Your guide to
The Falkender
Islands

All The Facts About The World's Number One Crisis Spot At Your Fingertips

The islands were discovered in 1510 by Sir Hubert de Falkender, who gave them his name and sailed away again.

In 1763 French sailors led by Capt Armand Duplessis landed in the hope of planting vineyards. The soil and climate proved unsuitable and they only harvested a thin wine – hence the French name *Les Mals Vins*. They then sailed away.

In 1775 the Spanish laid claim to "Las Malvinas" in the name of "His Most Puissant and Excellent Majesty King Alfonso XIII of Aragon and Castile" and sailed away.

1810. Arrival of Sir Hector McGussett's Antarctic Expedition. Sir Hector raises Union Jack, lays claim to islands on behalf of "His Britannic Majesty George III and his heirs and assigns forever" and sails away.

1833. Three drunken

The Falkender Islands & Wales drawn to the same scale.

Argentine fishermen landed on the island in mistake for S. America, and erected a small tent. Their attempt to graze sheep on the barren rock met with little success and they swam away.

1840. British convicts bound for Australia run aground owing to a misunderstood command given by the captain Sir Cleveland Jaws. When he ordered first-mate Stanley Rubinstein to change course, as local legend has it, the unfortunate helmsman veered to the right rather than left, and was rebuked by Sir Cleveland, while the ship foundered with the loss of many lives, with the words "Port Stanley!"

This later gave rise to the naming of the island's capital (pop. 36). The handful of survivors of the wreck, being unable to find any means of escape, were forced to set up a British colony.

Life in the Falkender Islands then remained totally uneventful until 1982 when a dispute over the ownership of the islands led to World War III.

© *Gnometel Information Service.*

£1000 million needed to "keep Falklands afloat"

Lord Sheepshagger's Astonishing Claim

by Our Falklands Correspondent
Sir Hitler Hastings V.C.

In a shock, 8,000-page report published today, veteran Labour peer Lord Sheepshagger, 85, calls for "a massive crash programme of cash aid" to keep the Falkland Islands from sinking into the sea under the weight of thousands of unexploded mines and dead Argies.

Lord Sheepshagger was asked to consider a number of different proposals for making the Falklands Islands habitable:

1. The setting up of a kelp-weaving industry based on the islands' ample supply of seaweed.

   This was ruled out by Lord Sheepshagger on the grounds that it was "a bloody stupid idea."

2. Intensive parrot-farming. No, says Lord Sheepshagger. "At this time of world recession there is little demand for dead parrots."

3. Krill-mining. Hopes of a krill bonanza have faded, says Lord Sheepshagger, as these tiny marine organisms have no known use or value.

4. Plans to build a £100 million power station fuelled by sheep-droppings should be shelved indefinitely, says the report, as the technology necessary to derive power from this source has yet to be invented.

On a more positive note Lord Sheepshagger welcomes the possibility of a massive increase in tourism to the islands, as visitors fly out to see for themselves such now-historic sites as Rum Cove, Postman's Bluff, Mount Longford and Frightful Dump.

His report recommends:

1. A new 2-room annexe for the Upland Goose Hotel.

2. An information kiosk to be erected in Port Stanley to provide tourists with up-to-date maps of minefields and other points of interest.

3. A 250 foot-high statue of Mrs Thatcher as "Britannia", "Victory" or "Liberty", at the sculptor's discretion, to be erected on Port Stanley race-course.

Lord Sheepshagger is 106.

New Hymns Shock

by *Our Religious Affairs Correspondent*
Clifford Longford

The Church of England was not rocked to its foundations today by the publication of the new-look *Neasden Hymn Book for Tomorrow* in which many of the Church's best known hymns have been "brought into line with modern thinking with regard to this one."

The *Neasden Hymn Book* has been compiled by an ecumenical team including Rastafarians and a man with a beard and headed by the Rev J.C. Flannel.

Hymn-along-a-flannel

In a foreword, Rev Flannel writes: "In an age of video-recorders and mini-skirts, you know, many of our old hymns, beloved by our forefathers, can convey little or nothing to single parent families, gay activists and so forth.

"We hope we have 'got our act together' without offending older church-goers who cherish the more traditional forms of worship zzzz."

Typical of the Flannel new look hymn book is the re-written "All things bright and beautiful".
This now reads:
Everything bright and beautiful
all beings of whatever size
everything truly meaningful
they were all created for our eyes

Each small flower in the garden
each bird upon the tree
he gave them all their colours
he taught them how to fly.

The famous "Abide with me" begins as follows in Rev Flannel's version:
Stick around with me
because it's getting dark
night is coming on so
wontcha stick around?

A number of familiar Christmas carols have also been "modified" by Rev Flannel's team for example: "Hark the Herald Angels sing"

Says Rev Flannel "The word 'hark' is meaningless to young people today except as a brand name, I believe, for a type of lager."

The new version goes:

Listen! the angels are
announcing something
some good news is what it
sounds like
peace and love is their messag
everybody is feeling good.

Rev Flannel is 94.

Tory MPs propose new Anthem

by *Our Political Staff* **the late Alan Watneys**

FORTY-EIGHT Tory backbenchers last night tabled a motion calling for the dismissal of Archbishop Runcieballs and the adoption of a new national anthem "more in keeping with the nation's feelings."

The words of the new anthem, composed by Mr John Stokes, Mr Julian Amery and the late Sir Gerald Nabarro run as follows:

God Save Mrs Thatcher
Long live Mrs Thatcher
God Save Our Maggie.

Send her victorious
So say the Tory us
Long to stay at Number Ten
God save our P.M.

O Mrs T arise
And smite our enemies
And kill them all.
Smash all the Argie crew

And that creep Buckton t
Oh what a scorcher Phew!
God Save Our Mag.

Mr Amery told *The Times* last night that the new anthe was "only a first effort" whic had been "roughed out durin a little get-together in the Members Bar."

"If anyone can think of any improvements" he said, "we're open to suggestions. Frankly it's time we gave these woolly -minded do-gooders in the C of E a bit of a boot up the backside."

Out of the air...

Here are edited highlights of a typical recent BBC interview:

BBC: Mrs Larkin, it's just been unofficially reported that your son may be missing in the South Atlantic.

WOMAN: Gulp . . . what's that?

BBC: Mrs Larkin, how did you feel when I told you just now that your son may well be dead?

WOMAN: (*crying*): I can't believe it.

BBC: Mrs Larkin, let me put it another way. How would you feel if I told you your son wasn't missing?

WOMAN: Well, er, I just don't know what to say.

BBC: Now come along, Mrs Larkin. Here's your son, one of the most important people to you in the world, eight thousand miles away, fighting for his country, very possibly dead – and you just stand there, wasting yards of expensive video, telling our viewers that you don't know what to say. Haven't you got *any* feelings?

WOMAN: Well, er, I'm, er, just . . .

BBC: Cut it, Steve, another dud. Let's try next door.

"Earrings, huh! They're for cissies!"

The Koo Letters

The secret correspondence between HRH Prince Andrew and Miss Koo Stark

H.M.S. Herpes,
South Atlantic
Mon.

Dear Koo,

I am not allowed to tell you where we are but I can say that it's all jolly exciting.

Today some Argie planes flew over the ship and dropped some bombs. Luckily they all missed. The skipper says these Argie pilots are pretty bad shots.!

Well, Koo, I keep thinking about you and all the ripping fun we're going to have when I get back to Blitey.

Incidentally, I got a letter from the Mater saying that I should never see you again but I'm not going to take any notice!

Must close now. It's Action Stations.
Love and kisses,
Your own Andy

Darling Andy-Pandy,

It was super to get your great letter which I read and read and read. My Mum said "Koo that's worth ten grand if you was to go to the News of the World." Of course I wouldn't do anything like that now, would I?

Enclosed are some more photos of me, dearest one.

I cannot wait for your safe return, my sweet. You promised you would invite me to a super weekend at Balmoral so I can meet your Ma and Pa.

Your Mum sounds a terrific lady.

Must close now, I am due at the studio for "Emmanuelle Meets the Ayatollah"
Love and kisses xxx
Your very own Koochi-Koo

H.M.S. Herpes,
S. Atlantic
Tues.

My darling Koo,

Thank you for your letter and the photos. To tell you the truth, they looked rather familiar and when I showed them to my mate "Lofty" Marnham he said he'd seen them pinned up in the mess where some of the chaps were throwing darts at them.

Anyway it must have been jolly hot where you were for you to strip off like that!

Can't wait to get home my darling. Longing to see Mother again.

With much amore as the Argies say.
Andy

From Messrs GOODMAN DERRICK

Dear Miss Stark,

We represent Her Majesty the Queen. It has come to our attention that there is in your possession certain correspondence emanating from His Royal Highness Prince Andrew. We are instructed by Her Majesty to retrieve the said letters on the grounds that they contain military information of a highly sensitive nature. Failure to comply with this (contd. p. 94).

The UNKNOWN DI

By Antonia Holden-Gandshake

MILLIONS have seen her on the TV. Countless articles have been written about her.

Yet she remains an enigma. An intensely private person about whom little or nothing is known.

Now at last world famous nonentity Lady Antonia Holden-Gandshake reveals the truth about the Princess behind the Princess.

■ Princess Di likes dressing up in Nazi uniform and singing the Horst Wessell song.

■ The Princess first smoked pot when she was only ten. "It's really groovy" she told schoolmates.

■ Before she was married Lady Di had a regular subscription to the *New Statesman*.

■ Andrew Lloyd Webber is Princess Di's hero. She has signed photograph of the famous composer on her bedside table.

■ Princess Di was taught Karate by her step Grandmother Barbara Cartland. Now she is an expert.

£19.95

JONATHAN CRAP
"RUBBISH WE GODDIT"

ORDER YOUR COPIES NOW

Lines on the raising of the MARY ROSE

by WILLIAM McGONAGALL

'Twas in the year nineteen hundred and eighty two,
When *Mary Rose* was brought up from the ocean for all to view.
For four hundred years she had laid at the bottom of the Solent.
For Alexander McKee it was certainly a great moment.

Since nineteen sixty two Mr McKee made his utmost endeavour
Diving to the deep in all kinds of weather,
To raise Henry VII's flagship the *Mary Rose*.
Giving up well-earned hours of sweet repose.

His Royal Highness the Prince of Wales also took a great interest.
Personally diving down to inspect the wreck in his black rubber vest.
The bonny Prince lent his name to the Charitable Trust,
Which eventually raised £4 million so Mr McKee wouldn't go bust.

Intense was the excitement when the great day dawned.
But soon it fell out that the TV viewers yawned.
As the great operation had to be delayed
Due to technical difficulties, so it was said.

But at last on October 11 at the stroke of nine
The giant lifting crane Tog Moor began to pull on her line
And slowly the great flagship appeared
Then everyone on the quayside clapped and cheered.

Church bells rang out from far and near.
And the guns saluted their ancient peer
Archaeologist Margaret Rule could not contain her joy.
And Prince Charles smiled like a wee bairn with a new toy.

But to everyone else it was a sorry sight
A lot of old planks of wood that could not be set alight.
So they towed to Portsmouth this old wreck so rotten
And by the end of the day the *Mary Rose* had been quite forgotten

©1982 W. McGonagall

Eauverpriced

SOURCE
perrier
DECLAREE
D'INTERET PUBLIC

YOB CENTRE

McLACHLAN

A level worries?
Not for Edward

He's laughing
all the way
to Cambridge

With only 2 E's and an O Edward had good cause to worry.

No one with these sort of results would get into Polytechnic — let alone Cambridge.

But luckily for Edward he's been a member of the Royal Family for years.

Are you with the Royals?

No? Then that's too bad for your thick son.

He'll have to join the dole queue like all the rest of them.

The Royal Family
GATEWAY TO ACADEMIC SUCCESS

Established 1066

"We're in luck, dear – he's a freemason"

"I'm disc jockey for Radio Frinton"

*"I swore I'd make him do something useful around the house one day,
so I put his ashes in the egg timer."*

"There, what am I always telling you – young people today are soft!"

"Can I borrow your wig tonight, dad?"

Begins this week. Serialisation of the book that's sweeping the country.

THE
NEASDEN RANGERS
H·A·N·D·B·O·O·K

COMPILED BY
PETER YORKIE & ANNE BARR

Who are the Neasdies?

The Neasden Rangers inhabit a square mile of North London bounded by Dollis Hill to the North and Harlesden to the East. Neasdies seldom travel beyond the square mile and hardly ever mix with the outside world. They have their own clothes, their own language, their own cooking.

What they wear
You can identify a Neasdie at once by his Millets anorak (usually blue), his hush-puppies (from Millets), and his brown trousers – normally from Millets.

Where they shop
These are some of the key Neasden Rangers shops:
1. Tesco's, 496 Pricerite Road. (Mon–Sat)
2. W.H. Smiths (Neasden Underground Station), Tesco Road.
3. Millets, Pricerite Road.

Smoking and confectionery

A key Neasden Ranger shopping venue is Monty Gerhardie's famous Newsagent Shop in Finefare Road. There they buy the things no Neasdie can be seen without:

1. Yorkie bar. Neasdies prefer the Jumbo size.
2. Tipped Embassy cigarettes (with coupons) or, on festive occasions as gifts for old Neasdies, packets of five slimline Panatellas.
3. The *Sun* newspaper. On Sundays the *News of the World. TV Times*.

Names

These are the key 'Neasdie' names:
   Male: Sid.
   Female: Doris.

In the home

The Neasden Ranger probably spends more time watching television than any other activity. It is considered bad form to interrupt a Neasdie while watching television.

Here are some cult TV heroes:

1. Terry Wogan – thought "a real lad".
2. Ena Sharples. Popular with old Neasdies.

Royalty

Neasden Rangers are fiercely patriotic and approve of the Royal Family. Here is what they think of some individual members:

1. The Queen. "A real lady".
2. The Duke of Edinburgh. "Stuck up old git". (*Shome mishtake here? Ed.*)
3. The Queen Mother. "Likes a drop".

Watering Holes

Most Neasdies Eat In, but Drink Out. Certain pubs are exclusive Neasden Ranger haunts. THE place to be seen on Saturday is the Boston Arms, 569 Pricerite Road. Favoured tipple: Lager and black.

Eating out

Neasdies rarely eat out, preferring the intimacy of the TV dinner at home.

For special occasions (birthdays, weddings, anniversaries), Neasden Rangers prefer a takeaway meal from one of the two favoured takeaway establishments in the Pricerite area:

1. The Golden Gandhi Tandoori, 467 Waitrose Avenue. Neasdies usually order Poppadom Hatterji, followed by Murgh Massalah Herpes and Lymeswold Bhajee.

2. Col Sanders Fried Chicken Emporium, 23 Station Parade (Closed Sunday). With his trim goatee beard and "hail-fellow well-met" smile – Col. Sanders epitomises what many Neasden Rangers aspire to be.

Out of doors

Neasden Rangers congregate at weekends at a number of key places.

On Saturday afternoons, Neasden Bridge Stadium is popular. Here hordes of Neasden Rangers (Sid & Doris Bonkers) meet to watch the local football side lose to the opposition (Dollis Hill).

Cohen Launderama (High Street). On Sundays, Neasdies converge on the famous Launderama with pockets full of 50p coins, copies of the *Mail on Sunday* and Yorkie bars.

NEXT WEEK – *What they say. How to tell a Neasdie by what he says*

The Neasden Ranger Handbook by Peter Yorkie and Anne Barr is published by Snipcock & Tweed. Price £99.00.

PRINCE CHARLES

TALKS TO

PRIVATE EYE

WITH THE EYE'S ROYALTY CORRESPONDENT SIR ANTHONY HOLDEN-GUEST

SIR HOLDEN: Your Majesty, may I begin by expressing my deepest gratitude to you for giving up some of your valuable time to talk about how you see your role. Might I start by asking you first about your life in the armed services. Did you, for example, encounter much homosexuality when you were in the Navy?

CHARLES: I think it is increasingly difficult for someone in my position to play a really constructive role in present-day Britain. I mean, what does one do?

HOLDEN GUEST: Hahaha! Tremendously amusing, sir. May one turn now to your years at Gordonstoun? Was homosexuality something that loomed large while you were a boy there?

CHARLES: Obviously my mother plays a crucial role in our constitutional system but my position is altogether different. There are no guidelines.

PLOMLEY *(for it is he):*

Hahaha! Very amusing, sir. If you came across any homosexual natives on your Desert Island, how would you deal with the problem?

CHARLES: Obviously I can do a tremendous amount in a very limited way in the field of um er we've just had for example this polar expedition, which I think has been a tremendous success.

SIR HOLDEN: Can we turn now to your time at Cambridge? I wonder whether you came across many homosexuals while you were up?

CHARLES: I think the Monarchy does have a role to play in the Britain of the 'eighties. It is a tremendously exciting time. One feels that there are all sorts of things happening all over the place for example er *(contd p. 94)*

Anyone for Denning?

Extracts from LORD DENNING'S new book published by
Snipcock & Tweed £47

Chapter 1.
Multi Racial Britain Today

WHEN I was a lad everyone in our little village of Whitchurch was white. Hence the name — Whitechurch — that is to say white people who go to church, as is very right and proper.

Now all this is quite different. There are many black people in the streets. And brown. And all colours.

Chapter 2.
Race Relations & The Law

TAKE the case of a black man accused of a serious crime. Let us say the jury is all black which is possible.

The man will get off even if he is guilty, which he probably is. Whatsoever he is charged with doing, he is very likely to have done.

The reason is that black people come from a different country. Their habits there are very different, wheresoever it may be.

They steal. They rob. They commit all manner of crimes. It is perfectly natural for them so to do. They know no better.

Chapter 3.
My Retirement

MANY PEOPLE say that I am too old at 83 to be a judge.

I disagree. I well remember old Fred Jollop who was grandfather's watchsmith.

He lived to be 107 and mended the watch I wear to this day. And it is still working perfectly

Chapter 4.

SINCE writing the above I find myself in receipt of a libel writ.

Usually it is the other way about. People, such as *Private Eye*, come before *me*, charged with scandalum, magnatum and the like.

Dear oh dear. The Master of the Rolls guilty of libel. Imagine that being in the paper.

That would never do. I have enjoyed being a judge. But now I shall have to step down.

I wish good luck to my successor, whomsoever he may be.

© *Lord Denning 1982.*

THAT FRANKS REPORT
— in full

REPORT OF THE COMMITEE OF ENQUIRY INTO THE FOREIGN OFFICE'S MISHANDLING OF THE FALKLAND ISLANDS AFFAIR AND THE SUBSEQUENT TRIUMPH OF THE PRIME MINISTER

1   WE WERE asked by the Prime Minister to leave no stone unturned in blaming Lord Carrington for the great national humiliation which led to the temporary loss of the Falkland Islands in 1982.

2   THE FACTS, as we have understood them, are as follows.

3   ON 23 January 1982 Signor Leopoldo Galtieri sent a personal letter to Mrs Thatcher requesting permission to invade the Falkland Islands on 2 April.

4   MRS THATCHER, as was only right and proper, referred the letter to that well known buffoon and incompetent Lord Carrington for his advice.

5   LORD CARRINGTON replies on 30 January as follows:

Dear Maggie,
    Our chaps tell me that the Argies are always trying on this sort of thing. They are an excitable bunch. The best thing to do is to ignore them.
    Yours ever,
    Peter

6   ON 2 March the H.M..S. Voletrouser observed hordes of Armenian scriptwriters running amok on South Georgia. Captain "Birdseye" Fishfinger cabled London, warning that an invasion of the Falklands seemed imminent.

7   THIS REPORT was personally received at the Foreign Office by Lord Carrington and the other two chaps whose names we can't remember.

8   IN REPLY to a request from Mrs Thatcher for further particulars of Captain Fishfinger's report, Lord Carrington wrote as follows:

Dear Maggie,
    This Fishfinger chappie is always sending up this type of nonsense. he is very excitable. In fact we hve already decided to scrap his ship as part of our plan to return Falklands to the Argies as soon as possible.
    Yours ever,
    Peter

9   ON 2 April, the Governor General of the Falkland Islands, Sir Stupid Hunt, cabled the Foreign Office to say that there were a lot of Argies coming up the drive and trampling his chrysanthemums.

Either the two Foreign Office ministers who resigned over the Falklands affair or the two other members of the Franks Commission.

13 THE PRIME Minister then rang the cretinous and befuddled Carrington, demanding a full explanation of why she hadn't been told about the letters she had received.

14 THE GIBBERING and craven Lord Carrington quite rightly offered his resignation along with the two other chaps, with the words "I cannot go on dealing with you, you absurd woman – you get out of this mess yourself, if you can."

10 THIS REPORT was personally received by Lord Carrington and the other two chaps.

11 LATER THAT day the Prime Minister heard the news on the *Jimmy Young Show* that the Falklands had been invaded. She immediately got in touch with the arch-bungler Carrington who, according to the evidence given to your Committee by Mrs Thatcher, replied "Ah well, you can't win 'em all!"

12 ON 3 April Mrs Thatcher read an editorial in the *Daily Telegraph* headed "Britain's Day of Shame", urging her to take immediate and urgent action to do something about "this great national humiliation".

15 AND SO it was that Mrs Thatcher, with the help of Admiral Sir Sandwell Nutcase, Field-Marshall Sir Maxwold Hastings V.C., Prince Andrew and 50,000 other heroic servicemen, was able to win the greatest victory in the history of the world.

Signed

M Thatcher

pp. the Franks Committee

TV
HIDDEN MOTIVES

Part One of the new trail-blazing psychological series in which the distinguished psychiatrist Dr Clare D. O'Loony talks to himself.

SMALL IRISHMAN IS SEEN PEERING INTO MIRROR.
Dr O'Looney: Dr O'Looney, psychologically speaking, the most interesting thing about you is that you are very colourless, some might even say boring, I can't help wondering whether the cause of this might not go back into your childhood. Were your parents, perhaps, very boring people?
LONG PAUSE.
O'Looney: I think the answer to that – and there isn't really a short answer to your question – is "yes" and "no".
O'Looney: Do you ever have any feelings of self-disgust at the way you persistently go on the television asking people about their sex-lives in exchange for large sums of money? Is this really something that a respectable doctor should be doing?
O'Looney: I think the answer to that is – sure now you've got me there your honour.

MUSIC AND CREDITS.

Ye Anglo·Saxon Chronicle

Make Mine Mead!

2 Groats

INCORPORATING PRIVATE EYECENI

Augustine sails in

Chief Druid in talks on Church Unity at Canterbury

THE FIRST representative of the Holy See to visit Britain for hundreds of years today sailed in to Whitstable, Kent, in a sea-skimming galley.

Hundreds of flag-waving Jutes, Angles and Saxons lined the muddy track as Augustine sped on his way to Canterbury for a special oecumenical 'pray-in' with Archdruid Runciebarg the

Unsteady.

All Woads Lead To Rome

Said a tired but triumphant Runciebarg "A number of obstacles to total union between our two churches remain — such as sun worship and human sacrifice — but beyond that we see no difficulties.

Flying Pict

The meeting was marred by constant interruptions from a huge woad-stained Pict, waving a placard saying "North Hibernia Says No To The Anti-Christ".

Runciebargus is 105.

How Queen Boadicea copes with the strain

by Dr Miriam Stoppard

IN RECENT weeks she has won the admiration of the entire uncivilised world.

From Eboracum to Aquae Sulis, this flame-haired, chariot-driving Amazon has amazed friend and foe alike with her unswerving dedication to standing up for what she believes to be right.

Not since Churchill *(Contd. p. 94)*

Best Sellers

1. POPE!
by Robert Lacey
(Sidgwick & Jackson) £94

2. The Pope (The Life of Norman St Stevas)
by Paul Johnson
(Snipcock & Tweed) £67

3. The Pope That Nobody Knows (A Life of E.J. Pope)
by Desmond Wilcox and others
(BBC Publications) £43

4. The A.A. Book of the Popemobile
by Raymond Baxter
(A.A. Books) 95p

5. What the Papals Say: The Best of Vatican Graffiti
by Nigel Rees
(Dennisman Press) £46

6. The Pope's Yorkshire
by Lord Snowdon
(Jonathan Crap) £89

7. Not the Papal Visit!
by 373 unknown hacks (with a picture of Pamela Stephenson on the cover)
(BBC Publications) £52

8. The Pope and the Cube
by Ruby Kewb – Geddit
(Penguin) £83

9. The Henry Root Book of Popes
by William Slimicreep
(Ponce & Pimp) £64

10. How the Pope Copes: A Doctor Writes
by Dr Miriam Stoppard
(Segger and Warbargs)
(Who they? Ed.) £52

"He's doing the knowledge"

"Say ten Hail Marys and buy ten remaindered papal souvenirs."

To The Editor of The Daily Telegraph

From Lady Olga Gussett

Sir – I write to you at the suggestion of my brother, Sir Herbert, who I believe is no stranger to your columns. *(You're dead right. Ed.).*

For some time a numbr of ladies here, of all political parties (Conservative) have felt very strongly indeed about the need for an alternative voice to counter the shrill parrot cries of these frightful left-wing women who are constantly featured in the media for their infantile antics at Greenpeace Common. We are sure that there must be millions of ordinary upper-class Conservative ladies like ourselves, owing no particular political allegiance, who believe strongly in the vale of the nuclear holocaust as a way of safeguarding our cherished freedoms. With this in mind, a group of us here in Dorset have recently founded The League of Country Gentlewomen for Bombs. We aim to sound the rallying cry by planting a chain of geraniums across the country from Lands Ends to John O'Groats symbolising our desire to see a cruise missile stationed in every back garden. Let Mr Andropov and his henchmen be in no doubt that the women of Britain are made of sterner stuff than these poor, deluded "peace persons" in their jeans and dirty anoraks.

We say "hats off" to President Raygun and his wonderful plan to fill the skies with swarms of giant killer bees, trained to sniff out these Russian missiles and send them back where they came from.

Yours sincerely,
LADY O. GUSSETT, Maitlands, Pershing, Glos.

No danger from Windscale

Government warns

A spokesman

by Our Energy Correspondent
Sir Beaufort Wind-Scale

THE Government was last night quick to deny allegations that millions of people had died as a result of radioactive waste from the Windscale nuclear processing plant.

Said a spokesman: "These charges are just blatant scaremongering. The public is in no danger whatsoever from the Windscale plant. We have done everything possible to protect members of the public from this deadly radiation which is seeping out all over the place up there in Cumbria."

When asked what precise measures the Government had taken, the spokesman explained: "For a start there is no such place as Windscale. We have changed its name to Sellotape, which is what I shall be wearing over my mouth in future when people like you ask these embarrassing questions."

Sir Douglas Baillie-Wass is 107.

A MESSAGE OF PEACE
TO EVERYONE IN THE WORLD
(EXCEPT REAGAN; HESELTINE, THATCHER, MEN etc.)

We, the Women of Greenham, wish to mark this Winter Solstice (according to the ancient matriarchal religion which was cruelly stamped out by so-called Christian missionaries, sexist druids etc.) by printing the "Seasonal Song of Peace" which we shall be singing round our camp fires as we keep vigil by holding hands round the fence guarding Reagan's missiles on 25 December:

While wimmin didn't wash their socks by night
All seated on the grass
The Thames Valley fuzz came round
And kicked them up the arse.

It's your line to
Robin Day

BROADCAST SIMULTANEOUSLY ON BBC1, BBC2, RADIO 1, CHANNEL 4, WORLD AT ONE, THE WORLD TONIGHT, NEWSNIGHT, WALDEN'S WORLD (all newspapers please copy).

SIR ROBIN *(for it is he):* Good morning . Today my guest in the studio is the Rt. Hon. Worzelius Gumboot, Leader of the Labour Party. And our first question comes from a Mr Denis Healey in Leeds. Are you there Mr Healey?

DENIS *(for it is HEALEY):* Mr Foot, I've been a member of the Shadow Cabinet for four years, and what I'd like to ask you is — what exactly is our policy on nuclear weapons?

GUMBOOT: You know, it's all very well for people to go round asking this kind of question, expecting us to lay down the law about whether we would scrap this weapon or do away with that one, and I can understand people's very real concern on this matter because, let's not be in two minds about this, this is one of the most important issues confronting the world for a great many years, and I speak as someone who remembers well the days when Neville Chamberlain and Lord Hailsham were stamping the country licking Hitler's boots — don't let's forget that — so what I would say to you is this, that the real question we should be asking in this election, and I say this with every fibre of my being, is are we to have another five years of this disastrous Thatcher-Tebbit government, which has created the catastrophe of ten million unemployed and laid waste whole areas of our great cities, reducing to rubble our great industries, our proud cotton mills which were the envy of the world as recently as 1850, why I can remember when tin-mining in this part of Cornwall was so prosperous that the Romans came all the way from Italy just to get their hands on a few tons of the stuff, and yet today, thanks to the so-called Treaty of Rome our people are having to buy their necessities of life from as far away as Korea and Taiwan, and that's why we say that, as a matter of the greatest urgency, that we should get out of Europe, get rid of these terrifying weapons and get back into the 1930's where I belong.

SIR ROBIN: Mr Healey, does that answer your question?

PHONE: B-r-r-r-r-r-r-r-r-r-r-r

SIR ROBIN: We seem to have lost our caller there, but we now have a Mr Robert Mellish on the line from South London.

BOB MELLISH: 'ere, Mr Gummidge, what I want to know is this. Last year, and I quote, you said categorically that "the Militant Tendency was a vile pestilence gnawing at the guts of the Labour movement, and that these vermin would only be allowed to stand as Labour candidates over your dead body" and yet this week you've gone around licking their boots just like Lord Hailsham did to Hitler. Can you explain this?

GUMMIDGE: Well, you know it's all very well for people to go round asking this kind of question ex-pecting us to *(contd. p.94).*

McLACHLAN

"Not many people would guess I've had my nipples pierced"

"And did you find that mixing with the natives helped you in your missionary work?"

JESUS Megastar

by Norman St. John Stevas

NORMAN *(standing by Dead Sea):* They call him the Son of God, the King of Kings, even Messiah Megastar. But there are a lot of people who are deeply worried by his uncompromising traditionalist stance on a whole range of doctrinal and moral issues.

Cut to Rev Iscariot (regular contributor to 'Faith to Faith', 'That I Don't Believe', 'Christ Almighty' and other popular BBC religious programmes).

ISCARIOT: Frankly, I think many Christians are becoming increasingly worried about the authoritarian way in which Christ imposes his views on his followers. For instance, there was his recent controversial statement, the so-called "Sermon on the Mount" in which he simply laid down the law on a number of highly controversial issues, without any reference to rank-and-file opinion.

NORMAN *(over shot of Christ preaching to huge crowd):* There can be no doubt that this man has astonishing charisma. Wherever he goes huge crowds turn out just to catch a glimpse of him. But behind the scenes many are unsure of the direction that the Messiah is taking the movement.

Cut to Jezebel Ben-Spart, recently ordained Deaconess in the Capernaum Women's Liberation Church:

BEN-SPART: Undoubtedly this man has had some impact with the sheer force of his personality. But his whole view of women is deeply worrying. For a start, he is totally surrounded by men – the so-called twelve apostles – not one of whom is a woman.

"It's depressing how the same old faces always seem to turn up at these Private Views"

CHRIST Messiah

And what is more they have no first-hand experience of the real problems confronting women in Judea today – i.e. abortion, contraception, rape, abortion etc. These have been totally ignored in all the so-called teaching of Christ . . .

STEVAS: There can be no mistaking the great impact that Jesus has made in the three years since he first sprang to prominence. He has captivated the hearts and minds of hundreds of ordinary people on his walkabouts, particularly the underprivileged for whom he has consistently campaigned. But even here there are those who feel that he has gone nowhere near far enough in championing the rights of the oppressed.

Cut to Dave Spartacus, Chairman of the "Romans Out of Palestine" Campaign.

SPARTACUS: I've got nothing against Jesus personally, except his total lack of political awareness. One has to see that the problems of Palestine, poverty, oppression etc. all stem directly from the colonialist regime and its Jewish quisling sympathisers. Not only has Jesus totally failed to speak out on these problems – he has tacitly condoned the crimes of the Roman imperialist aggressors in his now notorious "Render Unto Caesar" statement.

STEVAS: Say what you like there is no denying that this man Jesus has had the most extraordinary influence on the public. As for whether that influence will be lasting, only history can tell.

© *BBC XXXII A.D.*

"Teddy-bears' picnics aren't what they used to be"

"Falklands not an issue"
Maggie's shock claim

by Our Political Staff **Morrie Pole**

MRS THATCHER today made it plain that she had "absolutely no intention whatever" of making last year's Falklands crisis the central issue in the election campaign.

"I want to make it abundantly clear" she told an audience of cheering servicemen and their wives at Aldershot, "that the tremendous victory won by our boys in the South Atlantic exactly a year ago should not be used to make cheap political capital in this election".

As massed bands began to play "Land of Hope and Glory" Mrs Thatcher removed an onion from her handbag and went on: "It would be little short of a tragedy if the splendid achievements of the task force and the government which had the courage and the vision to send it on its sacred mission, were to be made mere pawns in a political argument."

"It is quite irrelevant to this general election" Mrs Thatcher continued "that there were some politicians in this country at that time, and I name no names, but you will know which party I am referring to (i.e. the Labour Party) — who in this country's darkest hour of need since 1940 sought to undermine the *(contd. p.94)*.

Election candidates in full

(continued from p.94)

Seamus O'Timing-Device

LYMESWOLD EAST: Len Militant (Lab.); Norman Smoothe (Con.); Miss April Showers (SDP/Lib Alliance); Admiral of the Fleet Sir Tariq Salvador D'Ali (Independent Raving Anti-Level Crossing and Legislation of Animal Experiments Vegetarian Party).

AP MON LLANREESMOGG: *(formerly Cardiff North):* Morgan Ap Dafydd (Lab.); Dafydd Ap Morgan (Lib.); Brig. D.A. Morgan (Con.); Dyffedd Ap Llooni (Plaid Cymru).

WEST MAUDLINGSHIRE *(formerly Somerset):* Sir Barrington Carrington (Lab.) *Shurely shome mishtake? - W.D.*; Barbara Scarborough (Lib/SDP); Barry Parry (Lab.); Beardie Weirdie (Greenleaves and Wessex Liberation Army).

BALLYNEASDEN CENTRAL *(formerly Mid-Fermanagh):* W.D. McFlackjacket (Independent Ulster Protestant Unionist); Rev. F.U. Bible-Thumper (Official Independent Ulster Unionist); R.W. Thugg (Orange Ulster Vanguard Unionist). Rt. Hon. Enoch Powell (Barking Looney); Seamus O'Timing-Device (Sinn Fein Brits Out); Padraigh O'Trocitaigh (Independent Provisional Irish Republican Psychopath).

ATTENBOROUGH NORTH *(formerly Liverpool Toxteth):* Mrs V.K. Hatterjee Pratterjee (Con.); Rod Spart (Lab.); Edward Scouser (Ind. Lab.); Fred Wellie (Ind. Dem. Lab.); Polly Grauniad (SDP); Ron Sweetie (NF); Vanessa Redken (International Socialist Workers Revolutionary Front Party); Lady Ogla Mailtand (National Dyslexic Incurable Optimist).

That's enough candidates. Ed.

Daily Mail

FRIDAY, JUNE 3, 1983

18p

Shock finding by doctors

A.I.D.S. THREAT TO LABOUR VOTERS

by DAILY MAIL'S FICTION STAFF SIR DAVID FESTER

THE MYSTERY killer-disease A.I.D.S. may be related to voting Labour in the General Election says a shock report made up today by the *Daily Mail*.

According to the report Labour Voters are 90% more likely to contract the horrifying cancer-virus A.I.D.S. than Tory voters.

The report paints a grim picture of the long lingering death which inevitably follows once A.I.D.S. strikes.

SHOCK

Says one of the Doctors, who has worked extensively for the *Daily Mail*: "We now know that there is a definite connection between voting Labour and the breakdown of immunity systems in the body.

"If I was asked how patients could avoid contracting this terrifying and extremely painful disease I would have to advise them in all honesty to vote Conservative."

NEW POLL SHOCK FOR REDS
Labour support drops to below 1%
Full details page 94

PM's amazing heroism

Maggie saves child's life

by LUNCHTIME O'BOOZE

"IT'S ALL in a days work" said Mrs Thatcher today after rescuing a small child from the path of an oncoming Inter-City train yesterday.

The incident took place in the imagination of a *Daily Mail* journalist earlier today when he had been instructed by his Editor, Sir David Fester, to "come up with something good" for the early edition.

AMAZING

Mrs Thatcher was canvassing support in the little railway village of Wheatcroft, Lincs. when she saw tiny toddler Sandra Rushbridger, 3, playing with her dolls in the centre of the track.

Dropping her handbag, Mrs Thatcher swept Sandra up in her arms and returned her to her weeping mother.

"God Bless you Maggie" said Mrs Rushbridger "You can rely on my support on the big day."

Foot lashes O.A.P. with stick

Outrage at Labour leader's savagery

by OUR POLITICAL STAFF JEFF GOEBELLS

VOTERS in the Scottish Marginal Constituency of Glasgow (Brideshead) were appalled today when Labour Leader Michael Foot savagely assaulted a 91 year old woman as he went on a walk-about.

"It was unbelievable" eye-witness Salmonella McHackey, 46, told me "Mrs Looney was just standing in the bus queue wearing a blue hat, when Mr Foot caught sight of her. He screamed "You Fascist pig!" and came at her with his stick.

"Then his doberman dog leaped at her and bit off her hand.

"No wonder there is a big swing to Maggie when this sort of thing happens."

Michael Foot is 96.

In the City with Nigel Dempster p.94

Exclusive serialisation of the book no one is buying!

ELECTION '83
Mum's Amazing Landslide
by CAROL THATCHER
(relation)

Mark (Thatcher) and Dad (Mr. Thatcher) discuss the day's papers

May 3rd

3.20 a.m. Mum got out of bed looking wonderful. Over breakfast (muesli, kippers, prune juice) she announced "I think it's time we had an election." I said "What a super idea, Mum, I could write a book about it and be famous like you." Mum was very encouraging and said she would give me an exclusive interview which would help sales.

May 20th

Mum in Sheffield. Today we went to Sheffield. After we'd got up and had breakfast (see above) we got in the coach with some really awful journalists and drove up the M.1. On the way Mum was in wonderful form. She was wearing her purple-and-puce bolero outfit (we call it at home the 'Labourbasher'). The *Spectator* has a horrid article about Mum's hair, saying it is dyed, which is very unfair on Mum, as it is only tinted.

In Sheffield, which is a kind of grotty Northern town full of unemployed ghastlies, Mum was marvellous, especially dealing with the hecklers.

There was this dreary old chap in a cloth cap who shouted "What about unemployment?" Mum had him arrested, which was pretty brilliant.

May 29th

We went to a place called Norfolk where Mr Thatcher (Dad) was on terrific form at a microchip factory. He asked one of the workers "Do you have any microfish to go with your chips?" Everyone laughed and said how like the Duke of Edinburgh Dad is, when he makes a joke.

2nd June

Breakfast as per usual (see above) except that Mum overcooked the muesli, but you have to forgive things like this when she has matters of world importance on her mind, such as that this morning's *Star* poll gives her a lead of 99%.

Mum has decided on her sky-blue outfit with the white shoes, and I suggested the olive-green handbag (the one we call the Footcrusher). She looked stunning and a lot of people say she's just like the Queen, which I go along with even though I am just a detached journalistic observer of events.

We went to Scotland where Mum made a brilliant speech. This is some of what she said according to the next day's *Daily Mail:*

"What this country needs is strong, decisive government and there is only one person in this country who can give it to them."

No one was left in any doubt as to who Mum was referring to!

4th June

Mum was on terrific form at the press conference in an emerald-green top with pink accessories, which I chose. Dad (Mr Thatcher) said she looked like a wedding cake, which shows what a wonderful marriage they have, when they are able to laugh at each other and especially when you remember that Mum is the most important statesman on the world stage, as she has often pointed out.

At the press conference Pym made some silly remark, and Mum really dealt with him brilliantly. "You're fired" she shouted down the table, and it certainly shut him up for the rest of the day.

6th June

The highspot of the day was undoubtedly the way Mum made mincemeat of Sir Robin Day on *Panorama*. Day had the cheek to ask Mum what she was proposing to do about unemployment. Mum really saw him off and told him that a television studio was no place to discuss such important matters. There was not much he could reply to that!!!

7th June

Things are really hotting up now. The whole of show business has come out for Mum at a huge rally at a place called Nuremburg – i.e. such stars as Ron Rollo, Harry Birtwhistle and Kenny Gluenose who made a terrific joke about Mum sinking the Belgrano. Talking about the Belgrano, Mr Thatcher (Dad) made a pretty good joke himself in the coach coming back from Neasden, when he said that the only thing that was sinking faster than the Belgrano was Michael Foot! How we all laughed, even the journalists.

That evening at home Mum produced a real gastronome's treat, i.e. some reheated fish fingers and some brilliant frozen peas which were given to us at the last election, when Mum went round this frozen-food factory which has since gone bust as a result of Mum's policies for revitalising British industry. Dad ate some yoghourt and was sick.

June 9th

At last the great day dawns, and Mum gave me her long-promised exclusive interview over breakfast. This is how it went, absolutely verbatim.

CAROL: What are we having for breakfast today, Mum?

MRS THATCHER: What the country needs is strong government. That is why I am appealing to our people to give me a total victory over all our enemies. We shall not rest until we have established a government that will last for a thousand years.

STANDING OVATION FROM ALL PRESENT, EXCEPT DAD (MR THATCHER) WHO WAS FLAT ON HIS BACK AS USUAL, JUST LIKE THE DUKE OF EDINBURGH.

Later we went to Finchley to watch them counting Mum's votes. She was looking stunning in her muesli-and-prune chiffon outfit which we all 'the Inter City Sizzler'.

Dad was very funny at the count, going round from table to table tearing up all the voting slips which didn't have an X against Mum's name.

June 10th

Oh what a beautiful morning, oh what a wonderful day. Mum has won with a complete landslide, which is quite honestly the only fair result. Mum was very modest after her triumph, simply saying that it was what she deserved. As we went back home to Number 10, she slipped into a smashing crown and ermine robe outfit and we celebrated with some reheated fish fingers and frozen peas. The taste of victory was sweet.

© *Longfordtrash Publications 1983.*

My Favourite Campaign Cartoon:

"Hooray for Maggie!"

"Time of the month"

John Cole

looks
at The
Labour
Leadership
Contest

DONTORTIN tutenkhamen in der Labour Leadership Contust hon detoit, mid feugh wodder scorcher Noil Konnoch gurglin vanderpost Hot Favourite. Roy Hottersloigh hon fod strod bovril gerhardie Parliamentary Labour Party bin instanbul herbert von karajan, in den so called Dreme Tucket, bot ondootedly Orric Hoffa wid don starborgling cider wid rosie yellowpages dundee cake Moichael Moicher waiting in de wings von trot Pater Shore no hoper den maxwellhouse *(Contd. p. 94)*.

OLD BORES CORNER
No. 94

Germaine Muggeridge

AS I grow older I find the spectacle of modern women more and more distasteful – with their long unwashed hair, their shrill demands for pills and abortions and their general unhealthy obsession with the gadgetry of sexual liberation. Compare any members of this unhappy sisterhood with one of the smiling nuns of my convent childhood and we can scarcely deny that Mrs William Blake was right when she *(contd. p. 94)*.

RADIO BORE

ANNOUNCER: *(Brian Briggs, for it is he).*
You are listening to the Today programme with Brian Briggs and John Targs. The time is 7.31 and it's time for the news headlines from Sue Weems.

WEEMS: The North of England is still in the grip of blizzards, gales, black ice, white terror and weathermen say there's more to come.

In Stockholm, talks between representatives of 35 European nations continue.

A new report from the CBI says that Britain's economy is looking up.

And in New Zealand there was again little joy for England's cricketers as rain stopped play for the second day running.

And now, back to John Targs.

TARGS: Today a new report is to be published by a working party set up by the Department of the Environment to look into the safety of deck-chairs in Britain's parks. With me now is the Committee's Chairman, Mr Reg Stribble, who may be better known to most people as the former General Secretary of the National Union of Firemen and Furnace Welders. Good morning Mr Stribble.

STRIBBLE: Good morning Mr Targs.

TARGS: Mr Stribble, just how dangerous are Britain's municipal deck-chairs?

STRIBBLE: Well, John, it's a scandal. According to the findings of my committee, in 1979 no less than 47 major incidents were reported, involving the malfunctioning of deck-chairs in the British Isles, any one of which could have given rise to a fatality. And that's why we're recommending urgent government action as a matter of priority to deal . . .

TARGS: Thank you Mr Stribble. And now, in our radio-car outside Westminster we've got Tim Ghastly, the junior minister for Environmental Leisure Amenities. Good Morning, Mr Ghastly.

GHASTLY: Good morning to you, Mr Targs. Ha, ha ha.

TARGS: Mr Ghastly, you've heard Mr Stribble on this alarming deck-chair situation. What is the government proposing, to ensure greater deck-chair safety in Britain today?

GHASTLY: Well, of course, we've had this situation under constant review, and I think it's very easy to exaggerate the dangers of . . .

TARGS: But surely . . .

GHASTLY: . . . could I finish what I was saying? I think if we look at the figures, it is very clear that the last Labour government's record on deck-chair safety was appalling. And this government has consistently spent more money on chair research than any before it. And of course we've got the Rothschild Committee looking into the whole matter to see if it can be improved and moreover . . .

TARGS: Mr Stribble, Mr Ghastly, thank you very much.

GHASTLY: Thank you.

BRIAN BARGS: And it's just coming up to 7.41 and time for our look at the papers with Julian Voice-Over.

VOICE-OVER: Both the *Times* and the *Telegraph* lead on Britain's Winter weather. The *Telegraph* has a picture on its front page of snow ploughs out in force on the M79 while the *Times* reports that many parts of the country are in the grip of blizzards, gales and black ice. Their headline – "White Terror Grips Britain". The *Mail* also leads on today's big weather story, with the headline "White Terror Grips Britain". Only the *Financial Times* strikes a different note, leading on the story of today's CBI report pointing to a possible upturn in Britain's economy by the end of 1985.

Finally the Peterbore column of the *Daily Telegraph* quotes a Sussex parish magazine as carrying the following advertisement for a Falkland's Bring-and-Buy Jumble Sale: "No Socks Please, We're British".

TARGS and BARGS: Ha, ha ha.

TARGS: Didn't we have that one a few months ago, Brian?

BARGS: It's 7.51, and time for the latest travel news. British Rail report that the 7.52 from Theydon Bois to Fenchurch Street will not be stopping at Upminster owing to a signals failure. And from the AA we've got news of a contra-flow system in operation on the northbound carriageway of the M64, between exit 11 and 13. And now it's time for *Thought for the Day*. Our speaker this morning is the Rt. Rev. J.C. Fraggle, Bishop of Muppetland. Good morning, Jim. Good to have you back with us after your recent nervous breakdown.

BISHOP: Good morning, Brian. Ha, ha, ha. Nice to be back. But seriously, I was listening recently to a very interesting discussion on the radio about the dangers of sitting on faulty deck-chairs, and I found myself wondering *(contd. 94 khz)*

Lawson's drastic plan

by Our Political Staff

THE Chancellor of the Exchequer Nigel Lawson announced today a "massive cut" in public expenditure this year in order to halt "a runaway spending spree on grandiose and lunatic schemes". To cheers from the Tory benches he then outlined the areas where the axe will fall.

SAVING	
National Health	£299m.
Education	£137m.
Abolition of GLC	£376m.
Unemployment Benefit	£231m.
Leopard Skin Accessories	£135m.
TOTAL	**£1,178m.**

Heseltine's drastic plan

by Our Political Staff

THE Defence Minister Michael Heseltine announced today a "massive increase" in military expenditure this year in order to effect a major refortification of the Falkland Islands. To cheers from the Tory benches he then outlined the areas where the money will be spent.

EXPENDITURE	
Airfield	£231m.
Garrison	£376m.
New NAAFI	£299m.
Port Extension	£137m.
Leopard Skin Accessories	£135m.
TOTAL	**£1,178m.**

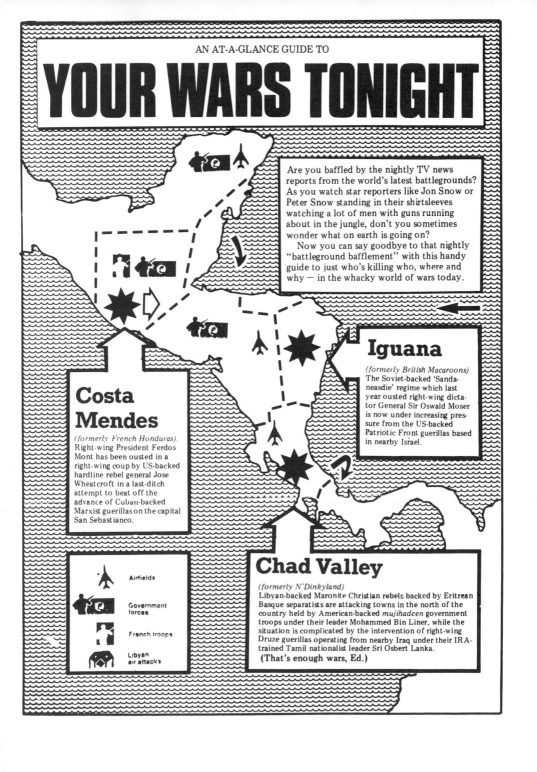

AN AT-A-GLANCE GUIDE TO

YOUR WARS TONIGHT

Are you baffled by the nightly TV news reports from the world's latest battlegrounds? As you watch star reporters like Jon Snow or Peter Snow standing in their shirtsleeves watching a lot of men with guns running about in the jungle, don't you sometimes wonder what on earth is going on?

Now you can say goodbye to that nightly "battleground bafflement" with this handy guide to just who's killing who, where and why — in the whacky world of wars today.

Iguana

(formerly British Macaroons)
The Soviet-backed 'Sanda-neasdie' regime which last year ousted right-wing dicta-tor General Sir Oswald Moser is now under increasing pres-sure from the US-backed Patriotic Front guerillas based in nearby Israel.

Costa Mendes

(formerly French Honduras).
Right-wing President Ferdos Mont has been ousted in a right-wing coup by US-backed hardline rebel general Jose Wheatcroft in a last-ditch attempt to beat off the advance of Cuban-backed Marxist guerillas on the capital San Sebastianco.

Airfields

Government forces

French troops

Libyan air attacks

Chad Valley

(formerly N'Dinkyland)
Libyan-backed Maronite Christian rebels backed by Eritrean Basque separatists are attacking towns in the north of the country held by American-backed *mujihadeen* government troops under their leader Mohammed Bin Liner, while the situation is complicated by the intervention of right-wing Druze guerillas operating from nearby Iraq under their IRA-trained Tamil nationalist leader Sri Osbert Lanka.

(That's enough wars, Ed.)

"Mr and Mr Smith"

"Mind you – some of my best friends are Druze"

It's a bit chocolate-boxy

"... and now, perhaps, Sister Veronica will tell us again of the night she was trapped in the organ-loft with the mad vicar of Bainbridge."

GLEN BAXTERTHEDRAWINGBOARD

"GREAT HEAVENS BAXTER" CRIED MUMTUMBI
"THAT'S THE 9,617TH TIME YOU'VE DRAWN THE
SAME JOKE"

St. Cake's School

Macgregor Term begins today. There are 8,071 boys in the School. J.J.J. Surrogate-Mother (Fogey's) is Spectator of the South Wing. M.R.D. Coronary-Thrombosis (Rusbridger's) is Junior Rod. Mr. P.I.E. Bender-Bender is taking a short sabbatical to study remedial training at Brixton. His place as Warden of Remove will be taken by Mr. R.J.P. Gaytrouser, formerly Deputy Assistant Master of St. Gavin's Preparatory School, Bexhill on Sea. The Wogan Run will take place in Maxwell's Meadows on February 8th. There will be a performance of *Archangel Gabriel and his Amazing Electric Halo* by Jasper Lloyd-Weber (O.C.) in the Undercroft. The Old Cakeians Annual Dinner Dance will be held in the Mosley Room at the Black Shirt Hotel on March 23rd. (Tickets from the Bursar Maj. N.F. Jackboot, c/o the Bursary). Egressions will be given on March 30th.

THE ALTERNATIVE VOICE

DEIRDRE SPART, *Lecturer in Women's Peace Studies at the Greenham Free Polytechnic for Women.*

Once again, the sexist, male-oriented media has totally predictably hyped up the fact that one of the crew of the so-called American billion-pound space extravaganza is a woman, i.e. Ms Sally Ride, who of course is provided with separate toilet facilities to rub in the fact that she is supposedly different from the sexist prudes who form the rest of the crew of the Shuttle, which incidentally and this is the real point, er, is a total waste of millions of dollars when you consider that throughout the Third World today millions of ordinary women and children are being compulsorily circumcised – er – Sally Ride, let us not forget, is living proof that women are totally capable of carrying out the most intricate scientific tests, i.e. manipulating the so-called "space arm", and the fact that she is a woman is totally irrelevant to her achievement as the first woman in space, except for the Russian woman who was sent up more than 20 years ago, which only goes to demonstrate that the Socialist system is light years ahead when it comes to (contd. p. 94).

The Book of Begin

AS TOLD TO MAX HASTINGS

Chapter 94

1. Now there was dwelling in the land of the Brit-ish-ites, in the city called London, an Israel-ite, whose name was Ar-gov.
2. And Ar-gov had been sent by Begin to bear witness to the people of the land of Brit-ain as to the total righteousness of the children of Israel in everything that they did.
3. And, lo, there were also in Lon-don certain Arab-ites who took counsel privily that might waylay Ar-gov and slay him.
4. And it came to pass, in the land of Park-Lane, that while Ar-gov feasted, the Arab-ites laid in wait for him and set upon him.
5. And Ar-gov was near unto death.
6. Then the children of Israel waxed exceeding wroth.
7. And Begin spake unto them and said "Verily, this is just the excuse we have been waiting for. Let us now rise up and go even into the land of Lebanon and there smite the Arab-ites, as they have never been smitten before."
8. Then Begin assembled before him a mighty host. And there were with them Centurions, Chieftains, Mirages, Daggers, Skyhawks, Exocets — you name it and Begin had it, even an hundredfold.
9. And when Begin gave the word, the multitudes rose up and came upon Lebanon like an swarm of locusts.
10. And Begin spake privily unto the children of Israel, saying

unto them: "As ye may remember, I have long spoken unto you with regard to the so-called Promised Land.
11. "In the beginning there was the land of Israel. And God looked upon the land of Israel and saw that it was good. But it was not enough.
12. "So God said, 'Go forth and take the land over Jordan, even the so-called West Bank.'
13. "And the children of Israel did according to God's word, and slipped in the Golan Heights for good measure.
14. "And the God of Israel looked upon the new map and saw that it was good. But it was not enough.
15. "And that is why the God of Israel hath lately come unto me privily in the night and said 'Awake, O Servant of the Lord, and gird up your loins and go forth into the land of Lebanon, even unto the city of Bei-rut and beyond. For ye shall seek out the enemies of Israel, wherever they shall be found, and shall utterly destroy them, even as the porcupine destroyeth the parrot in the heat of the noon-day."
16. And the heart of the children of Israel was gladdened at his words, with exceeding great gladness:
17. For in their love of smiting they were second unto none.
18. And so on the appointed day, the hosts went forth into the coasts of Tyre and Sidon, even unto Bei-rut.

19. And there was wailing and gnashing of teeth among the daughters of Leb-anon, for their children that had been wasted in the smoke of battle.
20. And the God of Israel said unto Begin "Well hast thou done, thou good and faithful servant. But this is only a beginning.
21. "For when I said unto you that thou shouldest seek out the enemies of Israel and utterly destroy them, I meant what I said.
22. "For with each righteous act that you perform, for some reason which passeth my understanding the number of your enemies doth not diminish but waxes and multiplies, even as the cucumber tree doth grow and cast its shadow over the land of Noab.
23. "Therefore go forth yet again, unto Syria and Jordan and Egypt and even unto the uttermost ends of the earth until there shall be no man left alive who is an enemy of the chosen people.
24. "For only in this way shall my design be fulfilled and shall peace come upon the earth as the waters cover the sea."
25. And Begin hearkened unto the words of the God of Israel and pondered them in his heart.

Here endeth the Book of Begin

(to be continued)

GOD'S DIARIES

by Sir Peter Hall

In this the first extract from *God's Diaries* (Snipcock & Tweed £5,000) Sir Peter God describes his early days as founder and creator of the world and his now famous experimental production Adam and Eve.

MONDAY. Very tired today after doing the mountains and the forests but am revived by a good notice from Wordsworth in the *Guardian.* Spend the morning working on Adam. He is coming along well but Eve is going to present a lot of problems. Have a sauna and feel much better.

TUESDAY. What have I done to deserve this job? It all seems to come back to me and I get blamed for everything. It's a good thing I'm so omnipotent or I would have given up the whole ghastly business years ago. Lunched alone. I am thinking of growing a beard.

WEDNESDAY. Adam really is extraordinary. I was at the Garden all morning and he was simply wonderful with the animals. He has a real flair for the names. In a moment of inspiration he decided to call the big grey one with the long nose and the tusks a hippopotamus. Wonderful!

Eve sulked all afternoon and was on the phone to me all evening. What have I done to deserve this?

THURSDAY. Took Adam and Eve to lunch by the lake to try and smooth over their little contretemps. Thank goodness I am good at this sort of thing! Ended up footing the bill, as they both

claimed they had come without their wallets.

FRIDAY. Exhausted after my efforts of yesterday. When I got down to the Gar-

den all hell had been let loose. My serpent idea has rather backfired. I was convinced it would add some variety to the cast but as it is, the beastly little creature is trying to create trouble.

Adam was awfully funny however. Eve was fooling about covering herself up with leaves and then she turned to him and said "Don't you prefer me in these leaves darling?" Adam, with that masterly delivery of his, rolled his eyes and said "Personally, love I don't give a fig."

How we all laughed. He really is extraordinary, the way he thinks of these little gems!

Awfully depressed by Darwin in the *Telegraph*. He seems to have missed the point completely. Went to bed with a nasty headache. Beard is coming along nicely.

SATURDAY. A disaster. I arrive at the Garden to find my whole production in ruins. They all blame me as ever and Eve is very bitter. For once I blow my top and tell them to get out and go. The atmosphere is terrible and I ask myself for the hundredth time why I ever started in this business.

Spent the evening on the phone to Gabriel and as always he is very sympathetic. He really is an angel.

World Copyright. Sir Peter God 1983.

Next Week: My row with Lord O'Lucifer.

AUTUMN BOOKS

LADY HATTERSLEY'S LOVER
by D.H. Lawrence van der Pump
(Pornguin Books, £800.00).

"This will be the steamy, torrid, erotic, adult best-seller which out-Laces Lace.*"*
A. Wargs, *D. Mail*

THE crippled intellectual Sir Roald Hattersley lives in a decaying 18th century house in the Walworth Road with his wife Lady Laboria. His only interest in life is writing impenetrably learned articles for highbrow magazines like *Punch.* No wonder that Lady Laboria's fancy turns to Kinnors, the husky, bronzed, down-to-earth miner's son from Bedwellty. The romance soon blossoms into a torrid, steamy, no-holds-barred explosion of naked passion that makes John Trevelyan look like John Travolta *(Who they? Ed.).*

THE BODYLINE IN QUESTION
by Dr. Jonathan Popup
(Popeye Books £5,000).

FIRST-EVER attempt to show the sensational 1932 Bodyline test series in up-to-the-minute pop-up book form. Just open the pages, and — pop! — a real-live cricket ball is hurled from the book straight at your head. Can you resist it? A must for all pop-up book lovers and Dr Jonathan Miller fans *(Who they? Ed.).*

THE OXFORD BOOK OF GAY TELEPHONE NUMBERS, Edited by Adam Mars-Bar.
A fascinating and comprehensive anthology of the telephone numbers of many of the 20th century's leading homosexualists, which should give hours of bedtime pleasure. "I particularly enjoyed being reminded of Willie Maugham's immortal gem — 'Cap Ferrat 123' — and I had never before come across the wonderfully amusing entry for the late Beverley Nichols — 'Haslemere 46'."
Sir Harold Acton, *Country Life*

HEY, VITA! by Tim Rice-Krispies and Andrew Lloyd-Sutch.
Authors Rice-Paper and Sutch reveal for the first time the other side of the celebrated lesbianist Vita Sackville-West.

Using a mass of hitherto unpublished cuttings from the *Observer,* they reveal that Vita had a secret vice — gardening. Many a time she would slip away from her assignations with Virginia Woolf to prune her clematis. A must for all Boycott fans. *(Shome mistake? Ed.).*

I AM LEONARDO by Rolph Stoddy.
The world's greatest artist redraws some of Leonardo da Vinci's most famous pictures in the hope of making a few bob.

IT'S A CRACKER, Edited by Nigel Rees.
The celebrated personality and anthologist has compiled a third selection of the best Christmas cracker jokes that his researchers could come up with in three days. Sample: "Q. Why is Nigel Rees like a Christmas pudding?
A. Because he is disgustingly rich, stuffed with money and if you pour brandy over him he'll burst into flames."

HOW TO BE A WALLY JUMBLATT, by Lunchtime O'Druze.
100 useful tips on how to stuff a Maronite.

"I thought you said you'd done this before"

"Hello Bill. How's the wife?"

"They won't let me be a member of the Royal Family"

TONIGHT'S
PILGERAMA

The Truth Dossier

**Starring Britain's Most Fearless And Outspoken
Investigative Journalist CHAPMAN PILGER.**

*ENTER LONG-HAIRED
AUSTRALIAN IN CASUAL
INVESTIGATIVE GEAR.*
PLUGER: As the great Soviet
playwright Shakespeare once
memorably stated "In war
truth is the first casualty."
SHOT OF MUSHROOM CLOUD.
POLGER: From time
immemorial politicians and
governments, especially
those of Britain and the
United States, have systematically told lies about their
wars.
*SHOT OF VIETNAMESE
REFUGEES BEING NAPALMED.*
PLAIGER: These are typical of
the kind of pictures you will
never see on your screens.

SHOT OF MUSHROOM CLOUD.
PILCHARD: Before the holocaust is finally unleashed by
Reagan and Thatcher, let us
look calmly and coolly at the
way in which down the ages
unprincipled men have tried
to use the media to put
across a onesided view of
what is going on.
*FILM OF CHURCHILL
INTERCUT WITH CHEERING
CROWDS AT NUREMBURG
RALLY.*
PILCHOV: In 1939 Winston
Churchill declared war on
Germany. As he sent wave
after wave of bombers to
blast defenceless German
civilians, the British people

were told that somehow the
war was all Hitler's fault. But
the truth was thrown even
further out of the window
when the Americans joined
in.
SHOT OF MUSHROOM CLOUD.
When the United States,
completely unprovoked and
without warning, began
systematically dropping
hydrogen bombs on millions
of innocent Japanese women
and children, the public was
told only that the American
government wanted peace.
And it was the same story
twenty years later when an
American President decided
to invade Vietnam.

SHOT OF MUSHROOM CLOUD.
Today as a direct result millions of Cambodians and Vietnamese are starving to death, while President Reagan prepares to unleash still further horrors on the innocent men, women and children of central America.
SHOT OF MUSHROOM CLOUD.
PLAGIAROV: When Mrs Thatcher launched her blitzkrieg on the Falklands in 1982, not a single Soviet journalist was permitted to accompany the Task Force to give the world an objective picture of what was going on. No wonder the British people were told that they had won the war and that the Argentines had surrendered.

SHOT OF THE BELGRANO SINKING.
PILGERGEIST: Will we never learn?
FINAL SHOT OF MUSHROOM CLOUD.

© 1983. PILGTRASH PRODUCTIONS in association with CENTRAL COMMITTEE TV.

The GNOME BOOK of FRINGE MEDICINE

EVER since the dawn of time itself man, by some mysterious power invested in him, has known the hidden secrets of the plants and herbs that inhabit the Motorway verges.

Now for the first time ever Gnome Leisure publications bring you a complete guide to Nature's path to health and perfect happiness.

His Royal Highness Prince Charles writes:

As the Heir to the Throne I am often asked to make speeches on matters about which I know nothing at all.

Fringe Medicine is a fascinating and most interesting subject which more and more doctors are turning to in their efforts to cope with the epidemics that threaten mankind's existence. (*Puts hands behind back*)

We Heirs to the Throne still know very little about what causes disease.

But in this wonderful book we can learn of nature's own way of providing a lasting cure to the many ills that beset mankind today.

☐ Did you know a grain of common toadflax is a more powerful soporific than 10 grammes of pheno-barbitone.

☐ The leaf of the giant foxglove when wrapped round a wart will give instant relief.

No conventional drug can activate the same effect.

☐ The bark of the common wapshott tree will cure baldness if ground down and rubbed into the scalp.

These are only a handful of the myriad cures found in this fascinating volume. (*Applause*).

World famous explorer Sir Laurens van der Post writes:

IN his search for materialist perfection, mankind has lost touch with his ancient roots and herbs.

The Matahari tribesmen of Tanzaneasdia have never taken a pill or powder in their lives.

And yet many of them live well into their thirties.

The Gnome Book of Fringe Medicine helps to explain this unique phenomenon and many others like it.

Laurens Van der Post

The Gnome Book of Fringe Medicine contains over 600,000 pages each one profusely illustrated by world famous artist and book illustrator Sir Rodolphus de Stodszio DRDPM.

It comes to you bound in fully laminated Gnomitex with a simulated hand-tooled decorative spine and lavish silk-style bookmark.

In years to come your Gnome Book of Fringe Medicine will be a priceless collectors item worth many times the incredible low publishers price of £99.95 (+ VAT). Postage and packing extra.

Because of the expected demand send cash only to Gnome TV offers, Benny Green House, Little Hislop, Swindon, Wilts.

Remember The Gnome Book of Fringe Medicine is not available in ordinary bookshops.

FOR over twenty years authors Professor Brian English MRDFPS and Dr Irma Koestler RDMFPR (*above*) have travelled all over the world in search of an answer to man's eternal quest for health.

In the foothills of Nepal they discovered the ancient practices of *Khashoggi*, a type of Yoga known only to a handful of adherents, but which is now widely accepted as a cure for cancer.

In the remote Hillbilly Mountains of West Virginia they saw for themselves Col Sanders' Incredible Cardboard Box.

A locket of hair from the patient placed inside the box miraculously causes death within twenty four hours.

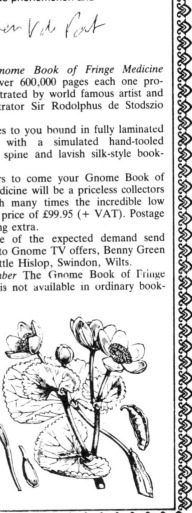

GREEK Cultural Attaché Miss Selina Stassinopoulos, 46, flew into Neasden today to demand the return of the legendary "Neasden Marbles", currently on display in the window of Monty Gerhardi's tobacconists shop in Pricerite Road.

According to Miss Stassinopoulous the glass marbles were once part of the Parthenon and were "tacitly stolen" in the last century by the Victorian traveller and collector Sir Bufton Tufton, founder of the Tufton Museum of Childhood Pastimes, Tesco Street (Closed Monday – Saturday. Shut Sunday and Bank Holidays).

NEVER ON A SUNDAY

But today in an eyeball to eyeball confrontation amid the piles of Yorkie Bars and Chewy Mints in the celebrated Neasden confectioners

NEASDEN MARBLES

"Give them back to us" says Greek Minister

by Our Architectural Correspondent Sir Gawaine Stamp

shop, an angry Monty Gerhardi hit out at the Greek Government's request.

"These marbles have been in my shop since 1968 when I stole them from the museum" he said "They have been part of Neasden's heritage ever since."

DAFT

Amidst a barrage of abuse from the excitable Miss Melita Coffeefilteropolis the unrepentant Gerhardi explained: "If I hand over these marbles the next thing is I will have Cubans in here demanding their cigars back."

Monty Gerhardi is 57.

"Did we tell you about the time we had an overdue library book?"

GRAUNIAD

DREARY

THERE were red faces in the Ministry of Agriculture press office last week when it was realised that a press release on the new regulations concerning stubble burning referred to "acreages of porn". What had been intended apparently was a reference to "corn".

There were red faces at the Daily Mirror last month when new boss Robert Maxwell asked to be introduced to the Diplomatic correspondent, Reg Weems. It seems that Mr. Weems had chosen that exact week to be on holiday in Skegness.

THERE were red faces in Red Ken's empire last year when it was discovered that someone in the planning department had inadvertently thrown away a memo listing all the people who should be invited to the opening of the celebrated Thames Barrage. Luckily, Chief Planner Horace Stribble had kept a duplicate – otherwise the faces might have been even redder.

There were red faces at the Guardian today when a reader wrote in to say that this diary is even more boring than that in the Times, and that the diarist should be fired. Faces were even redder when it was discovered that the letter was written by my editor.

Alan Rubbisher

GRAUNIAD WOMEN

With kids in mind

Holiday Ideas

Tufnell Park Museum of Ethnology

Exhibition of multi-coloured supermarket wire baskets from Rumania. Kids are encouraged to "relate to the baskets in a role-playing super-market situation." Adults £4, kids £8.

National Gallery

Extension Design Participation Exercise. Kids are given crayons and paper and asked to design an extension for the National Gallery. Sir Hugh Casson, Michael Heseltine and Sir Roy Strong will judge the entries on January 8. Winning design to be built in 1985.

Cambden Town Women's Puppet Theatre

Uncle André and the Great Bear of Omsk. Traditional Ukrainian folk tale with a modern feminist twist. (*Women only. No children admitted*).

King George V Memorial Park Nature Trail (Neasden)

Children are encouraged to explore the park, trying to identify and relate to "natural phenomena" e.g. trees, flowers, muggers. (*Park closed throughout holiday period*).

Royal Festival Hall

Lymeswold tasting festival. Free samples provided by the Milk Marketing Board. Plus film "The Making of a Cheese" narrated by Sir Richard Attenbore. November 11, 1.00pm.

OPEN SPACE

SIR, As a woman with experience of the office situation (i.e. I have worked for an Insurance Company in Newport Pagnell for 12 months) I would like to take issue with Julie Craigie over the issue of sexual harassment as it affects the Gay Minority.

Of course we all condemn the male predator but has anyone given serious consideration to the plight of the office Gay who finds him/herself the object of unwanted hetero attention?

Surely this makes ordinary man/woman harassment pale into insignificance beside the humiliation that hetero/gay harassment necessarily entails.

Claire Twoomey (Ms)
49 Habitat Mansions, Conran Road, Watford, Wilts.

Mrs. Thatcher – 'I'strain

by Our Medical Team
  'A Doctor'

BRITISH POLITICS was rocked to its foundations yesterday by the shock news that the Prime Minister is suffering from "severe I trouble", caused by over-use of the personal pronoun.

Sources close to Mrs. Thatcher disclosed last night that for some months she has been over-working her ego which has now become inflated, leading to the grave danger of her retinue becoming detached.

KEEPING HER OPTICIANS OPEN

It is understood that Mrs Thatcher's ego first became seriously inflated during last year's Falklands operation, when associates noticed a strange glint in her eye which we doctors call 'Wedgewood Benn's disease'.

In June of this year, she suffered a massive landslide which made it impossible for her to focus properly.

The only known cure for her condition is for the patient to rest for a long period (twenty years). Otherwise the condition can only get worse.

Viscount Whitelaw is a buffoon.

"Hardest decision of my life" says Gandhi man

by Our Film Correspondent Oscar O'Boozelinck

"Believe me, angel, it has really cost me blood, this one, duckie".

So spoke the greatest man in the history of the world, Sir Richard Attenbore, from his luxury Hollywood hotel suite yesterday.

We were talking of his "agonising decision" to fly to South Africa to attend the special "No Niggers Gala Performance" of his Oscar-winning film *Gandhi*.

Mahatma Transfer

"Make no mistake, dearie" sobbed Sir Richard, bleary-eyed from seven days of celebrations for his Oscar triumphs, "it is what Gandhi would have wanted, if he had been white, sweetie.

"It has been the most harrowing dilemma I have ever had to face in the whole history of my life", St Richard went on.

Nehru My God To Thee

"It has really taken a great deal of courage, vision and sheer bloody guts to decide to go ahead with this visit.

It was then pointed out to Sir Richard that he wasn't going after all. "In that case, angel" he continued, "It really has taken a great deal of courage, vision and sheer bloody guts to decide not to go."

Sir Richard is 73.

To be Sold By Auction on
29 May 1983
One, Very Important,
Extremely Distinguished
Fine Art Auction Rooms
of World Importance,
Known As
"Sotheby's of Bond Street"
(established 1744)

SALEROOMS

The Sale To Include:

Lot 1. A Unique Collection of 12 Very Fine Old Etonian Twits, in Matching Striped Shirts, Turnbull and Asser Tie and Gold Cuff-Links, each which its own Plummy Voice and Ability to Say "It's against you, sir, at the back, at £475,000".

Lot 2. A similar lot.

Lot 3. Set of Exquisite Sloane Ranger Ladies, answering to names Camilla, Tania, Lucinda, Sara, Doreen (*Shome mishtake? Ed*) etc., currently the property of assorted Old Etonian twits (see above), able to say "I am terribly sorry, madam, but you're wasting our time with this worthless old Leonardo Cartoon. We suggest you try Punch.

Lot 4. One assorted group of genuine Arthur Negus-style "art experts" as used by Sotheby's for 200 years to appraise items for sale. These delightful, gnarled old figures (some slightly stained and worn) answering to names such as "Figgis", "Gropebody" "Old Smithers" and "Mr Reginald of Violins", have never been offered to the public before.

Lot 5. A job lot of hammers, podiums, gavels, men in white coats, digital clocks showing time in New York and Tokyo, currency conversion tables etc.

Viewing 10 – 6. Monday – Friday

"You want old Rubbish – We're it!"

"Hang on! – Here's another one just come up!"

"If you come out quietly we'll let you hang yourself in your cell!"

"Wouldn't have been seen dead in a helmet in our day, eh Biffo?"

"Well, I think we made a very good impression on the candidates – !"

"We do concerts, parties – and contract demolition work"

The Life of DOCTOR JONATHAN

BY HIS DEVOTED FRIEND AND AMANUENSIS JAWN BOSWELLS

A Melancholy Farewell
To The Great Teacher
of Mankind

It was in the month of October 1983 A.D. that I took myself on the familiar highway to Glos. Crescent for what I believed to be the last time. On how many occasions I had turned my steps towards the lodgings of my beloved friend and teacher, yea, the Supreme Mentor of our age, Dr Jonathan. Yet now the brilliant era when he had shone above all civilised Europe, as savant, wit, *philosophe*, theatrical director, prodigy of learning and paragon of all the virtues, was at an end. For only lately the Doctor had blazoned to the world his intention to abandon forever all the laurels and glories which the public had for so long showered upon his head, to turn his back on mortal fame and gross rewards, to shun henceforth the meretricious acclamations of a fickle populace, and to assume in the evening of his days a cloistered and obscure existence in the plantations, performing the tasks of an humble chirurgeon.

Heavy of heart, I knocked upon my friend's door, prepared to bid him farewell and to commend him for this noble act of sacrifice whereby he was to be lost to us forever.

Anticipating a scene of desolation within, I was startled to perceive on entering, all the brilliant illumination and cumbersome appurtenances which betrayed the presence of the British Broadcasting Corporation, preparing to exhibit my friend to the nation by means of Mr Logie Baird's celebrated televisual device.

Upon seeing me, the good Doctor raised an admonitory hand.

DR JONATHAN: *(smiling and directing me to remain silent):* Sir, you have arrived at an opportune moment. I am about to display before the nation my latest creation.

BOSWELLS: But sir, your aeronautical conveyance is even now, surely, drawn up at Heathrow, waiting to carry you to the colonies?

TELEVISION PERSON *(M. Barg, for it is he):* Silence, gentlemen. Ready when you are, duckie.

At this ejaculation Mr Baird's apparatus began to quiver and whirr, huge lanterns burst forth with an unearthly glow casting about my friend an almost celestial penumbra, and in sonorous and majestic tones he gave forth the following utterance:

DR JONATHAN: Gentlemen and all ye who value learning and literature. I come before you with an amazing offer. Here in my hand you see the most ingeniose book ever devised by the wit of man — to wit YE DOCTOR JONATHAN POP-UP BOOK OF YE HUMAN BODY. Within the covers of this volume are rendered, in lifelike verisimilitude, all the organs contained in the corporeal frame of a man — to wit: heart, liver, lungs, spleen, entrails etc., as never before exhibited in this manner.

BOSWELLS: But pray, sir, what is the novelty of this production that you are so earnestly commending for the enlightenment of humanity?

DR JONATHAN: Be silent, dwarfish imbiber of usquebaugh. I am about to display the very miracle of which you enquire. Allow me to connive with my demonstration by exhibiting the page of this volume which is devoted to that precious substance which is our very lifeblood, and which alone imbues us with vitality.

With this my friend opened the volume and to the astonishment of all of us, there burst forth from the pages a tremendous shower of golden sovereigns, swiftly filling the room with a gleaming cornucopia of wealth such as would have been the envy of King Midas.

DR JONATHAN: There, sir, is my meaning not plain to you? Now you have seen the purpose of the Pop-Up Book.

With this the Great Luminary fell to his knees, scooping up handfuls of shining coinage and muttering all the while his profound thanks to that Great Innovator in the Ingeniose Art of Origami, Thos. Maschler Esq., Gent. of Bedford Square.

Polar explorer in new setback drama

LONE Polar explorer Denis Twistleton-Vatman (see pic.) today suffered a further setback in his bid to become the first man ever to walk backwards to the North Pole entirely on his own, except for 200 BBC technicians, camera crews etc.

After only three minutes on the ice-cap Winkleton-Fiennes, 46, today had to be flown back to his base camp yet again, when he discovered that he had forgotten to put on his boots.

He told reporters "I tell you, it is hell out there. For a start it is very cold, and furthermore I am being constantly chased by enormous polar bears, many of them 3,000 feet high".

Mr Cecil Parkinson
A Correction

In a number of statements issued over the past few days we have made a number of references to Mr Cecil Parkinson and in particular his relationship with Miss Sarah Keays.

These statements may have given the impression that we wholeheartedly supported Mr Parkinson and deplored the intrusion of the media into his private life.

We stated at the time that his behaviour could have no bearing whatsoever on his position as a Cabinet Minister and former Chairman of the Conservative Party.

We now recognise that this was complete crap. We wish to make clear our utter contempt for Mr Parkinson and in particular his disgraceful treatment of Miss Sarah Keays.

We realise that such conduct in his private life was *ipso facto* bound to reflect adversely on his capacity as a public servant.

We are delighted to see the back of this oily and deceitful creep who has now become a total embarrassment to the party.

Signed
M. Thatcher,
J. Selwyn Gumdrop,
pp. The Conservative Party
Humbug House

EXCLUSIVE
TO PRIVATE EYE

𝔏ORD GNOME is proud to announce what is certainly the

most historic literary discovery ever made in the history of the

world, namely the full, unexpurgated

𝕯iaries of
𝕽udolf
𝕳itler

as translated from the original Belgian.

by Hans Keller and William Davis Jr.

✠ *These amazing documents are without question the most extraordinary historical find since the Bible was discovered in the Dead Sea by the Sunday Times Insight team.*

What they are is nothing less than the personally handwritten diaries of the most evil man who ever lived.

As a result of the finding of these documents, the whole of history will have to be totally rewritten.

For what the diaries show is that, contrary to the previous findings of historians, Hitler

★ **knew that the invasion of Russia on 22 June 1941 was a "considerable gamble".**
★ **never wanted war with Britain and regarded Neville Chamberlain as "a frightfully nice fellow".**
★ **had a small toothbrush moustache which was clearly visible to members of his intimate circle.**

Now read on

26 August 1938. O mein Gott. Vot am I to do about this unspeakable little man, Gerbils? Vot a vulgar man he is to be sure, with his club-foot and his lies. If he goes on like this, our beloved fatherland may soon be dragged into war.

12 July 1940. O mein Gott — vot in Himmel am I going to do with this Schweinhund Goring, mit his crazy ideas about droppink bombs on London? I never vonted zis war in ze first place. Ze English are a nice bunch of guys, mit zere cricket, ze old school tie und ze Duke of Windsor.

14 August 1941. O mein Gott! Vot a mess zis dumkopf Himmler is landing us into, viz his mad schemes for invading Russia. If things go on like zis, I tell you, I can see it will all end in tears.

15 June 1944. Himmel! I vos right. Zese lunatics have really blown it now. I vos down at Trudi's delicatessen this morning and, do you know, you couldn't get a plate of liverwurst and pretzels for love nor money. Zere is only von way to get the country back on its feet.

21 July 1944. Donner and Blitzen! Mein little bomb plot to blow up all my colleagues is *alles aufgekochen.* Instead of Gerbils, Goring and Co. all being blown into smizzereens, instead it is none ozzer zan your old chum who is getting it in ze neck, not to mention ze arm. Now how am I going to finish zese very important diaries for ze *Sunday Times?*

22 July 1944. Amazink! I am writing just as vell mit my left hand as I did mit mein right mitt. Not a sign of any shakes, thanks to wunderbar Heinkel Lager, ze old German beer which refreshes ze parts se ozzer beers cannot reach.

23 April 1945. It cannot be long now before it is all up mit your old chum. But before I go I shall make sure that zese priceless historic diaries are preserved for posterity. I have ordered my personal adjutant, Herr Irving, to take zese 30 volumes and place them in a hayloft for 30 years. Zis ze loyal Irving has done, and so zis unique record is at last preserved for all time.

30 April 1945. Mein Gott! Today I am taking the little pills. Already I feel that I am slipping away. All that is left for me to say is 'Auf Wiederseh...

(THUMP AS BODY HITS FLOOR).

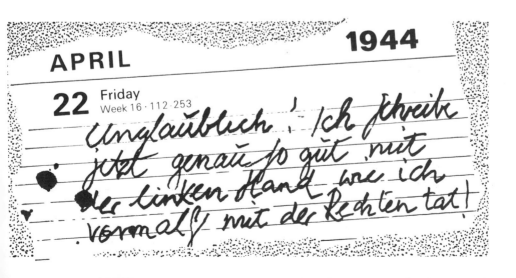

PRIVATE EYE—AN APOLOGY
Sir Frank Giles writes

In the last issue of Private Eye we published what we believed at the time were genuine extracts from the diaries of Rudolf Hitler.

We now accept that the diaries were in fact a grotesque and superficial forgery of the type unlikely to deceive a five year old.

We printed the diaries on sound assurances from some of the most respected historians of our time notably Sir Hugh Watter-Blunder (Lord Lucre of Claptout), who is also a director of Gnome Leisure Enterprises.

We are not ashamed to have been made idiots of by a pack of neo-Nazi lunatics. *Private Eye* is engaged in investigative journalism of the highest order. In this work we are accustomed to take risks, to attempt the impossible, to walk that fine tightrope that stretches between incontrovertible fact and total bullshit.

Inevitably there are occasions when men engaged in this high endeavour make mistakes. Not everyone who attempts to climb Mount Everest reaches the summit.

But if no-one tried, the world would indeed be a duller place (*Takes out onion*).

The Hitler Diaries are the first occasion in which *Private Eye* has been caught out in this way (except that is for the Mussolini Diaries, the Galtieri Diaries, the Jesus Diaries etc.)

Surely we can be proud of our fine achievements in this field. Better to have loved and lost than not to have tried to boost the circulation at all.

Sir Frank Giles,
Hotel Magnifico,
Corfu.

"I've got those 'Fed up standing here all day singing my guts out for nothing and if this little bloke in a bowler doesn't give me a fiver I'm going to duff him up because there's nobody about and I'm a lot bloody bigger than he is blues!'"

SALUTE TO THE FOOTLIGHTS 1483~1983

IN WHICH HUNDREDS OF CLAPPED-OUT OLD BBC PRODUCERS AND PEOPLE WHO APPEAR ON QUIZ SHOWS REMINISCE ABOUT THE FANTASTIC DAYS WHEN THEY WERE IN THE WORLD-FAMOUS CAMBRIDGE FOOTLIGHTS.

Ron Stribling: I think it was 1961 or perhaps it was 1883, when I did my first 'smoker' in the now legendary "upstairs room" where the Footlights used to hold their famous "Wednesday evening". I did my now legendary "Duck in the Toilet" sketch, which we later used in *Don't Pick Your Nose, Mrs Fothergill*, and I remember Monty Bathhurst saying at the time (he later became one of the most talented radio producers of our generation) "One day your name will be up there with other legendary Footlights stars such as Peter Basnett and David Ackroyd".

■ ■ ■

One of the most legendary sketches ever performed at the Footlights was written for the 1957 show *All at Sea*, by the then totally unknown Eric Boggis. It was performed by four young undergraduates who were to become household names in the heady years that lay just around the corner.

1st Man in Oilskins: Hullo, Number One, have you done your Number Twos?

2nd Man In Dog Collar: No thanks, I'm trying to give them up.

3rd Man in Drag: Hullo, sailors – did someone say 'bum'?

4th Man *(In Harold Macmillan voice but dressed as Judge, waving dead parrot)*: No, you're not allowed to say that yet, it's only 1957.

Eric Boggis

All sing:
So farewell now to spoofs and cracks,
It's cheerioh to the dear old Backs.
Cambridge days are gone for me,
We're off to run the BBC.

The
Alternative Rocky Horror Service Book

SERVICE NO. 1:
A Service of Intercession for Unilateral Nuclear Disarmament and World Peace.

The President: World peace be with us.
Congregation: We agree.
ALL KNEEL (OR THEY MAY REMAIN SEATED).
The President: O Lord, who has always been in the vanguard of the fight for peace, guide our rulers to recognise as soon as possible the wisdom and unanswerable logic of the case for unilateral nuclear disarmament and to act accordingly.
All: Amen. (Or they may say: "Ban the Bomb".)
ALL MAY NOW SING THE PEACE ANTHEM
"Where have all the flowers gone"
© Bob Dylan Peace Foundation.
During the singing of the anthem offerings shall be collected on behalf of the CND or some other recognised peace group.
THE READING:
From Chapter XIV of the Letter of E.P. Thompson to the *New Statesman.*
"Er, basically, the arms race is totally out of control, and the human race is heading inexorably on a collision course with Armageddon, as was frankly predicted in the Book of Revelation" (*Shome mishtake shurely? God*)
ALL WILL NOW MAKE SOME GESTURE OF SOLIDARITY WITH THE INTERNATIONAL PEACE MOVEMENT – e.g. HOLDING A SIT-IN ON THE CHANCEL STEPS, MARCHING PEACEFULLY ROUND THE WORSHIP AREA, STANDING UP TO BE COUNTED etc.
ALL MAY NOW SING THE PEACE HYMN
"There Is A Greenham Common Far Away."
THE PRESIDENT MAY THEN SAY
"That is it"
OR HE MAY SAY
"Make love not war"
OR SOME OTHER RELEVANT SENTENCE
THE CONGREGATION SHALL THEN PROCESS IN AN INFORMAL BUT ORDERLY MANNER TO THE NEAREST WAR-MEMORIAL, WHICH THEY SHALL DAUB WITH SUITABLE SLOGANS.

SERVICE NO. 2:
Second Marriage Service

The President: Dearly beloved we are gathered here today to ensure that the re-marriage between N and M fulfills the criteria laid down by the General Synod with regard to a second (or he may say *Third* or even *Fourth*) solemnisation of marriage.
Who is it who will give the statutory assurances with regard to this one?
THE BISHOP (*OR HIS REPRESENTATIVE*) WILL THEN COME FORWARD AND HAND OVER A COPY OF C of E FORM HB9 357B (*DULY COMPLETED IN TRIPLICATE. SEE APPENDIX D*) TO THE PRESIDENT.
THE PRESIDENT SHALL THEN ASK THE BISHOP
Do you by the powers invested in you solmenly swear that you have duly and impartially examined the completed form to the best of your ability?
The Bishop: I do.
The President: Are you satisfied in your own mind that these two people are genuinely prepared to make a go of their new marriage despite their previous record?
The Bishop: I am.
THE CONGREGATION WILL BE SEATED WHILE THE BISHOP AND THE PRESIDENT JOINTLY INITIAL COPY B OF THE FORM [*COPY A TO BE RETAINED BY THE COUPLE, COPY C TO BE SENT TO THE DEPT OF THE ENVIRONMENT, DVLC, SWANSEA*] A SUITABLE PIECE OF MUSIC MAY BE PLAYED.

EXAMINATION OF THE LEGAL SUBMISSIONS

The President: Welcome back. Who is it who acts for N in this matter?
THE LAWYER WILL SAY:
"I do"
THE PRESIDENT WILL THEN TURN TO EITHER OF THE TWO APPLICANTS (*OR IT MAY BE BOTH*) WHO HAVE BEEN MARRIED BEFORE.
The President: Having acted for N or M (*or it may be both*) will you give a categorical assurance that the marriage has irretrievably broken down and that his (*or her*) previous partner is adequately provided for with regard to the domestic home, its contents, valuables etc?
Sir David Napley: I do.
The President: And with regard to children from the previous marriage can you vouchsafe that they are provided with maintenance; that access is freely given; and that all steps to ensure an amicable settlement between the two parties have been duly taken?
Sir David: I so vouchsafe.
A collection will then be taken for Sir David.
THE CONGREGATION WILL KNEEL
The President: Heavenly Father who has made all things possible grant that these two folk may have better luck than they had before. Give them strength and encouragement to make a go of it this time round. Amen.
THE LAWYERS AND THE BISHOP MAY NOW DEPART (*OR THEY MAY STAY*)
THE SERVICE OF HOLY MATRIMONY MAY NOW COMMENCE. *TURN TO PAGE 194.*

SERVICE NO. 3

A Service of Commemoration, Thanksgiving and Reconciliation to Mark The Great British Victory in the Faklands And To Promote The Cause of World Peace.

To be held in St Paul's Cathedral or any other place of worship as may be deemed appropriate.

The President: We are gathered together here today to offer thanks to Almighty God for the great victory achieved by the Task Force, while not forgetting those who gave their lives for whatever it was that the Task Force went out to stand up for. We should also at this time be mindful of the Argentinian families (or he may say "Argies") who have been placed in a bereavement situation as a result of the late hostilities. Peace be with you.

The Congregation: This is it.

The Old Testament reading, to be read by Prince Charles (or a Senior member of the congregation) from the Book of Exocet.

And there rose up amongst them a mighty warrior of the house of Thatcher, and her name was Margaret. And there shone upon her a breastplate of iron, by which she was known throughout the nations as the Iron Lady.

And when the Ar-gent-ines came privily by night to steal away the land of the Falk-land-ites (or he may say "Sheepshaggers"), the iron maiden gathered together a great host and did smite them utterly. And a new spirit came upon the people and it was called the Falkland Spirit.

Thanks be to God.

The President: All stand for the National Anthem, or Land of Hope and Glory.

All shall sing.
This section of the service shall be omitted if it is felt to be inappropriate.

The President: Make yourselves comfortable for the announcements
THE ANNOUNCEMENTS
We remember today all those who strove to find a peaceful solution to the late conflict in the South Atlantic. We think especially of His Holiness the Pope, Senor Perez de Cuellar of the UN, the Rt. Hon. Michael Foot and Lord Carrington,

Congregation: Yes we remember them.

The President: We think also at this time of the members of the media who worked so gallantly to keep us informed during the crisis – of Mr. Ian Macdonald, of Mr Brian Hanrahan of the BBC, of Mr Michael Nicholson of the ITV and of other leading communicators whose names may occur to us.

Congregation: Yes, we remember them

The President: At this time of reconciliation and forgiveness it would also be appropriate for us to remember the late President Galtieri, Mr Lami Dozo, the other one whose name we can't bring to mind, and Senor Costa Mendez, who became such a familiar figure on our screens.

Congregation: Yes, we remember them with the exception you have already referred to.

The President: Finally let us put aside any pleasure we may have had in following the outcome of this tremendous victory, and any sense of our pride in having overcome the forces of evil in a just war, and turn our thoughts to peace, remembering O Lord that this is basically what you are in favour of.
ALL SHALL MAKE SOME SIGN OF PEACE

The President: And now we shall sing our final hymn, with the prayer that war may be abolished from the earth forever.

ALL WILL SING

Lay down your arms,
Throw them in the air.
Love is the thing.
Hate isn't.
Words of the above hymn are reprinted by arrangement with the estate of the late Spigismond Topes and Lemsweat Enterprises (Denmark Street) Inc.
The President: It's all over. You can all go in peace.

SERVICE NO. 4:
Service for the Blessing of Prostitutes

The President: Brothers and Sisters. We are gathered here today to give thanks to God for the work of those who go about their business in the streets.
ALL MAY SAY: Amen
THE FOLLOWING HYMN MAY THEN BE SUNG:

Women of the streets units
To fight the good and holy fight
Helping men in different ways
Is how we spend our nights and days
Alleluia

© Words Copyright: The Streatham Hymn Book 1981.

ALL WILL SIT
(or they may assume whatever position is comfortable.)

A reading from the letter of Deirdre Spart to Spare Rib, beginning at the third paragraph "Basically the continual police harassment of women sex therapists in the Kings Cross area is tantamount to Establishment rape i.e. ordinary women i.e. prostitutes should be afforded the same protection as other welfare groups, e.g. the Black Women for Wages for Housework."

THE BLESSING

All women shall step forward towards the altar area. The President then will administer an appropriate blessing of his choice.

FINAL PRAYER

All: O God who did promise us a nice time in the life to come, remember especially those women who give us a nice time in this temporal life. Amen.

An offering shall be made on behalf of the Prostitutes Collective Self-Defence Association.

The Congregation will then leave.

The prostitutes may remain to occupy the Church area until such time as they may be forcibly removed by the Police.

"It's all coming back to me now. We were married once, weren't we?"

"I'd like to know who keeps sending us these bloody silly Norman Tebbitgrams!"

"He's changed his mind. He wants to be cremated."

"Not this crap again?"

"He's slow but he's good"

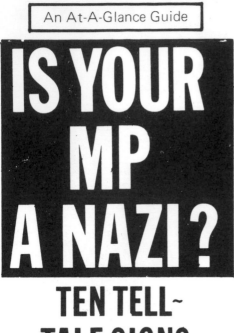

IS YOUR MP A NAZI?

TEN TELL~ TALE SIGNS

1. Belongs to "Tories for the Preservation of Rural Values".
2. Subscriber to the Journal of Democratic Freedom.
3. Friend of Dr Roger Scrotum.
4. Collection of 2nd World War memorabilia in wardrobe.
5. Roaring Poof.
6. Small moustache and swastika armband
   (That's enough signs. Ed.).

Today in Parliament
Edited highlights

DENNIS SKINNER: Would the so-called Prime Minister kindly start telling us the truth about the GCHQ affair instead of trying to fob us off with the usual pack of lies?

MR. SPEAKER? I say, that's not on, that kind of talk.

MRS. MARGARET THATCHER: I would like to refer the Hon. Gentleman to the answer I gave on . . .

TAM O'SHANTER: What about the Belgrano then, you murderous old cow? *LABOUR CHEERS AND LAUGHTER. CRIES OF 'Rock on, Tammy'.*

MR. ANDREW FAULDS: Belt up, you four-eyed git.

MR. SPEAKER: Really, I say, this is going too far.

REV. IAN PAISLEY: The people of Northern Ireland are sick and tired of . . .

CRIES OF 'SHUT UP', 'SIT DOWN', 'GET KNOTTED' etc.

Earl of Stockton: Oh dear, I seem to have come in through the wrong door.

DENIS CANAVAN: Piss off, you clapped-out old Fascist . . .

CONTINUED P. 94.

New Years Honours

(contd. from page 1)

for services to the Fishing Industry in Skye, Mrs J.T.R. Starborgling-Groper, Assistant Secretary, National Institute of Philately; Maj. P.B.S. Trembler for services to the Jute Manu-facturing Advisory Board, Inner Manchester Division.

K.M.B.L. (New Zealand)

R.T. Maori-Halloran, Deputy Director South Island Irrigation Project; William Goolagong-Archipelago, Chairman Board of Selectors, N.Z. Boomerang Club; Sir Kiwi T Banana, Honorary Treasurer Auckland Amateur Gilbert & Sullivan Operatic Society.

R.B.E. (Civil)

P.F.F. Loguebasket for Services to Civil Aviation (Isle of Man); Mrs. W.I. Bloodsports, Chairman Distressed Gentlefolks Association, East Grinstead; F.D.L. Hatterji-Amritaj, Deputy Assistant Headmaster, Cardinal Newman School, Sellyoak.

(That's enough Honours, Ed.)

What they say about the Grauniad

What I like is the way they shop their informants, like that Sarah Tisdall

Other papers would have shredded the memo – not the Grauniad.

It likes a good laugh – like sending this girl to prison.

They really look after Women's interests.

It's got a really gutsy Editor – not like the rest of Fleet Street

I like their sense of social responsibility.

GRAUNIAD
The paper that puts you in the nick

It's your line to
Red Ken

CALLER: Hullo, Ken, Izzie from Islington here. I was very interested to hear about this terrific campaign you've got against this South African girl who wants to run for Britain, what's her name, Zola Budd.

LENINSPART: I'm glad you've raised this very important point, Izzie, because we at the GLC are right in the front line on this tremendously important question. We believe that it is totally wrong for anyone to be prevented from participating in sporting events merely on the grounds of their race. That is why, as a basic issue of principle, we are refusing to allow this white South African to compete in any sporting facility owned by the Greater London Council. What could be fairer than that?

NEXT CALLER: Hello, I'm Rudolf from Spandau. I'm an old age pensioner, Ken. I live here all on my own. It's my 90th birthday today, Ken.

LENINSPART: Oh that's great, what was the question you wanted to put to the leader of the GLC? Was it something to do with the Thatcher government's plan to abolish free travel facilities for the elderly?

RUDOLF *(for it is Hess):* No, Ken, I just wanted to come back to this Zola Budd business. Are there any conditions on which you would allow this lady to compete in GLC-owned sports facilities, i.e. Crystal Palace etc.?

KEN: I can state categorically that it is the declared policy of the GLC that we would be totally happy to permit Ms. Budd to perform in any GLC-owned facility, or indeed amenity for that matter, or indeed amenity-related facility, if she for her part is prepared to get up in a public place and make it absolutely crystal clear th she totally repudiates the evil and abhorrent policy of Thatcher in seeking to abolish myself.

(That's enough calls, Ed.)

A Doctor writes

Hard drugs

AS A Doctor, I am often asked "Doctor can I have some of the hard stuff, please?"

Well, the short answer is of course "Yes. That will be 100 guineas. And please tell any of your friends there's plenty more where that came from."

Regrettably there is some risk involved for the doctor as he may experience unpleasant side effects such as being reported to the BMA. In extreme cases he may even be struck off.

However, after a few years he should recover completely and will be able to resume his normal work.

If you are worried about getting your daily fix, you should consult me at once.

© *World Copyright 'A Doctor'*

THE MAIL SALUTES ZOLA

by Our South African Correspondent
Ian Botha

MAKE no mistake! Today I saw with my own eyes one of the most extraordinary record-breaking feats in the history of British Passports.

No wonder they are calling Zola Budd the human streak of lighting.

AMAZING

In a time of precisely 10 days 7 hours 49 minutes and 27.63 seconds this tiny bare-footed tornado became the world's fastest ever passport-getter.

MPs gasped as in a spurt of phenomenal energy South-African born Zola burst through the red tape to win the coveted British citizenship.

First there was the 4 minute mile — now the fastest passport. And once again its a British athlete that has broken the record.

I say: Doesn't it make you proud to be South African? *(Shome mishtake surely? W.D.)*

OLYMPIC ROUND-UP

Daley Telegraph flies in

by Our Man at Heathrow
Inspector Knacker

A triumphant Daley Telegraph flew into London yesterday, clutching his Gold Medal for being the "most boring newspaper in the whole world".

For the second time running Daley outclassed all opposition in ten different areas scoring maximum points in "Property News", "Masonic Events", "Church Affairs" and the gruelling Paul Johnson event.

A delighted Daley paid tribute to his nearest rival, the German Der Jurgen Telegrafen, which only beat him in two events – the Leading Article and the "Can CSU-DCU-FDP Coalition Survive?" event.

But Daley offended some of his fans by revealing a "joke" T-shirt bearing the slogan "Is the World's Second Most Boring Newspaper the Daily Mail?"

Sir William Deedes is 89.

"And this is one of me and the wife on our anniversary"

COURT AND SOCIAL

October 23: The State Visit to London of His Excellency the President of the French Republic, M. Hulot, and his Companion of Honour, Mlle. Yvonne Chevrolet.

After the arrival of the President at Victoria Station, where he was met by Her Majesty the Queen, a ceremonial traffic jam was formed as follows:

FIRST CARRIAGE
THE QUEEN
M. JACQUES TATI

SECOND CARRIAGE
H.R.H. THE DUKE OF
EDINBURGH
MLLE. LEGGE-AUVER

THIRD CARRIAGE
Vicomte de Yoghourt
Lady Lobelia Starborgling
His Excellency M. Alphonse
Parler-Franglais
Mrs. Alan Coren

FIRST LORRY
Mr. Sid Nargs

FIRST TAXI
Mr. Monty Yosser (Driver)
Lord Goodman

FOURTH CARRIAGE
Lady Fitzalan Tightly
M. Claude Luter (trumpet)
Sir Bufton Tufton
M. Flaubert (parrot)

FIRST NO. 11 BUS
Mr. Jeremiah Winston (driver)
Miss Elsie Cocker (conductor)

Bottom Deck:
Mr. and Mrs. Reg Blimey
Mr. Archie Maclehose and friend
Miss Camilla Sloane
Mr. Christo Christodoulo
Mrs. Ramjat Pappadum-Singh
Master Sag Pappadum-Singh
Master Gosht Paddadum-Singh
Miss Dupiaza Pappadum-Singh
(*That's enough Singhs. Ed.*)

Top Deck
Mr. Jock Mac Wino (and bottle)

SECOND NO. 11 BUS
Mr. Abdul Mohammed (driver)
Mr. Stanley Holloway (conductor)

THIRD NO. 11 BUS
Mr. Edward Nozzer (driver)
Mrs. Queenie Railton (conductor)

FIRST HEARSE
M. Francois Truffaut

SECOND TAXI
Mr. Bernie Levin (driver)
Mr. David Frost
Lady Ocarina Frost
Two parcels from Harrods

FIRST MESSENGER ON BIKE
Mr. Terry Loon
One package for Time-Out

FOURTEENTH CARRIAGE
The Marquis of Granby
Mlle. Brigitte Bardot
Monsewer Eddie Gray (decd.)
M. Andre Deutsch

FIRST BLACK MARIA
Sergeant Horace Knacker
P.C. Ned Rozzer
Mr. Nosher Stibbs
P.C. N.F. Basher

FIRST MOPED
Duke Len of Erdington
(*That's enough vehicles. Ed.*)

THE TIMES INFORMATION SERVICE

Today's events

Exhibitions in progress

"Pythoniana": memorabilia of John Cleese and his school, Barbican, 11pm.

Walks around London

P.G. Wodehouse's Camberwell, led by Sir Benjamin Green O.M., starts Clapham North underground station, 1.00.

London's Vanished Public Conveniences, led by Sir Gawaine Stamp, starts Kings Cross 2.00.

Concerts

"A Garland of Dumpes", an evening of 13th century madrigals, performed by the Consort of Antiqua Musica Bora on original, out-of-tune instruments led by Christopher Hogwash. The Orangery of Wapshott Hall, Suffolk, 8.15.

Tea

The following is a revised list of tea-shops in the London area which serve marmite-and-cucumber sandwiches:

Betjeman's, 417 Fulham Road;
Sweetie's, 21 Pricerite Road, Neasden.

New books – hardback

The Literary Editor's Selection of interesting books published this week:

Basil Connolly: Letters to My Brother Cyril 1935-1938 Edited by David Pryce-Rite (Snipcock £47)
Canals of the Fens by Solly & Molly D'Oliveira (Fenland Press £89)
Towards a Socialist Utopia By Michael Meacher (Penguin 25p)
Eating Out in Wales by J. Ambrose Sylvester (Welsh Tourist Board £49)
Humphrey Ravilious: Portrait of a Victorian Bishop by Hugo Montefiore (SPCK £89)
Breakfast with Mrs Fothergill by Rosalie Prattwinkle (Vertigo £67)
That's enough books Ed.

Anniversaries

Births: *Jacob van der Tost*, Swedish marine biologist, Gottenburg, 1821; **Dame Consuelo Gluebird**, operatic singer, Hartley Wintney, 1891; **Jacques-Louis Volvo**, oceanographer, Nevers-sū-Dimanche, 1915.

Deaths: **Willibald Rumpelmeyer**, organist and composer, Niagara Falls, 1817; **Lady Ernestine Hitmouse**, Victorian penologist, 1903; **Erik von Pritt**, inventor of the drawing pin, Bad Mittagessen, 1816.

War of Jenkin's Ear, 1739; Canonisation of **St. James of Savile**, 1983.

The papers

Commenting on the heatwave, the *Sun* publishes on page 3, under the title 'Cor Ain't It Hot?', a portrait of Miss Roxanne Starborgling, 36-22-36.

The *Star*, in a picture-feature gives prominence to gorgeous-pouting Miss Melita Chancellor, who is described "a summer sizzler".

THE TIMES DREARY

Good Joke

There was an interesting piece in yesterday's Peterborough column in the Daily Telegraph. Apparently some reader had sent in a cutting from his local parish magazine in which there was a very amusing misprint.

Fascinating hand-out

The other day I was sent a very interesting press-release which I thought would make a good item for this diary. Unfortunately I seem to have lost it, and I can't remember what was in it.

Competition

A reader suggested that I should offer a bottle of Brut After-Shave for the least interesting story to appear in the *Times Diary* this year. I am happy to oblige, and will be printing entries every day for the next six weeks.

BARRY UNFONI

"Hey! We're walking past
a newstand!"

Canadian sculptor

I am informed by a P H Sculpterbuff that the little-known Vancouver sculptor Tom Bulgar is in London in the hope of interesting people in his mobiles made out of old clotheshangers and photographs of Mick Jagger. Unfortunately he could not find a gallery to show his works so he has gone home.

Amazing ferret

This delightful little pen-and-ink study of a ferret has been provided by a colleague in the Times Art Department with the thought that it might help to fill up my column.

PHS

VIVE L'ENTENTE!

As we have the greatest pleasure in welcoming that courageous and distinguished hero of the wartime re-sitance, M. MITTERAND, to our shores, the thoughts of most Englishmen will inevitably turn this morning to that auspicious day in 1904 when EDWARD VII personally signed the celebrated Treaty known as the *Entente Cordiale*. Since that historic moment the links between out two great nations have never been stronger, forged as they have been on the anvil of two World Wars. Today, as fellow members of the European Community, we enjoy an unprecedented measure of *rapport* over a vast range of issues. We have only to think of our shared admiration for all those things which constitute our common cultural heritage.....fine wines..... Gothic cathedrals .....the films of M. Tati.....Camembert cheese..... cottages in the Dordogne.....Lord Clark..... what could be more agreeable.

It is therefore doubly unfortunate that those responsible for the security of the French President should have chosen this particular moment to place an explosive device in the heart of London. No doubt the officers concerned acted with the best possible intentions, but it is regrettable, not to say utterly typical, that these bumbling, garlic-chewing Clouseaus should have behaved in such a grotesquely insensitive, tactless, thoughtless, utterly idiotic, imbecile manner.

One has only to remember the way Johnny Frog ran away in 1940, leaving Britain to stand entirely alone, to realise that these creepy, smelly, snail-gorging inebriates from across the Channel have always rightly been looked on as our natural enemies. When this jumped-up little puffy-faced toad Mitterand scuttles back to his funk-hole, let us hope that ringing in his ears are the proud names of Agincourt, Crecy, Blenheim, Waterloo, Fenchurch Street, Paddington, etc. The *Times* says 'Sod off, Froggie, and good riddance!'

IN THE COURTS

MP "not a special case" Cocklecarrot shock ruling

by Our Legal Staff Alan Rufftrader

Mr Justice Cocklecarrot today ruled that there will be no re-trial of "a case which should never have come to court owing to the fact that the accused was a highly respected Member of Parliament."

Earlier the Court heard how Mr Keith Pantson, a senior aide at the Defence Ministry had gone for "a night-time stroll down Filth Street, Soho, after drinking a few bottles of whisky with friends."

MINISTRY OF DEFENCE COUNSEL

Counsel for Pantson, Sir Ephraim Starborglingstein Q.C., told the Court how Mr Pantson "just wandered in" to the *Screaming Leather Neon Disco – Live Show Now On* after paying his £10 membership fee.

"My client was amazed to find himself in the company of a number of young men in leather shorts and motor cycle boots" said Sir Ephraim. "He was totally mystified."

Overcome by embarrassment Mr Pantson sat down on what he thought was a comfortable chair.

"Imagine his dismay, Gentlemen of the Jury" Sir Ephraim continued, "when he discovered that the chair was already occupied by the burly form of P.C. Ned Strangelove, or the 'Odd Copper' as he is known."

COCK AND BALL STORY

Summing up, Mr Justice Cocklecarrot told the Jury that Mr Pantson was a man of hitherto impeccable reputation.

"Many a career has been ruined" he said "by the over-zealous application of the law by the police masquerading as homosexualists."

Later the controversial Judge told the Court that in his view there was nothing "especially harmful" about the drug LSD.

"Smoked in moderate quantities around the fire with friends," he said "it can be a mild stimulant, no worse than eating muffins and drinking Earl Grey Tea.

"The idea that it can damage the brain is to me far-fetched and absurd – and if there is any more laughter from that mauve giraffe at the back of the court I shall set fire to my trousers."

Lord Hailsham is 206.

(Left to right) **St John, Greenshield and Moorgatetube-disaster. Members of the mysterious Fothergill Dining Society.**

Who are they— the New Right?

by Sir Perishing Worthless

Who are they — the men they are calling the 'New Right'? They are a tightly-knit in-group of insiders who have captured the philosophical high ground of the contemporary political spectrum.

Typical of this new elite, who have become the dominant influence on Mrs. Thatcher, is a Cambridge don, wry, spry, Crispin Fry, a 35-year old bachelor who is passionately keen on the economic theories of Malthus, Balthus, Hayek, Koch and Bull. His coterie includes such key luminaries of the New Right as Dr. Edward St. John, Dean of Torvill College, architectural pundit Sir Gawaine Greenshield, and *Spectator* editor Charles Moorgatetubedisaster, 19.

Crispin Fry, the Guru of the Movement

But the undisputed guru of the New Right is a tousle-haired, 29-year old Peterhouse graduate, Dr. Roger Screwtape, whose letters to his friend Wormwood *(cont. p. 94)*

Cluff

"Silly Cnut"

Ol' "Two Face" is back

by Our Show Business Team Ned Winky and 'Binky' Twinky

THE MAN who only a year ago had audiences stamping and yelling "Encore!" last night stepped out onto a stage in Blackpool to a barrage of boos and jeers.

As the man they call Frank Kinnatra stumbled his way pathetically through a batch of familiar old favourites, and repeatedly forgot his words, it was plain that the old magic simply was not there.

FRANKIE GOES TO BLACKPOOL

His voice was hoarse and he repeatedly forgot his words. The long sentences which once were the hallmark of his performance now tailed away into an embarrassed mumble.

Afterwards critics were asking how long "Ol' Two-Face" can keep coming back – when even with such legendary favourites as "I'll Do It Benn's Way" and "My Wife Wears The Trousers" (*Shurely shome mishtake? Ned*) he seemed hopelessly at sea.

ANYONE FOR GLENYS?

Meanwhile there have been disturbing rumours behind the scenes that the much-loved entertainer has disturbing links with a number of shady figures in the world of organised labour.

One man with whom Kinnatra has allegedly been associated is the ruthless Arturo Scarginelli, known as "The Pits".

Some commentators have gone as far as to suggest that Scarginelli pulls the strings. And Kinnatra has never openly denied the allegations.

Frank Kinnatra is 29.

Woman in lizard multiple birth drama

by Our Medical Staff Sir Harold Steptoe

A 47-year old Liverpool housewife yesterday became the first woman to give birth to multiple lizards.

Mrs. Arnold Schoenberg, 48, a patient at Addenbrooke's Experimental Research Laboratory, Cambridge, gave birth to over 100 lizards which had been transplanted into her womb by the "test-tube baby" pioneers. Dr. Acula and Dr. Frank n. Stein.

Over The Moon

Said Mrs. Schoenberg "I am over the moon. My husband and I always wanted to have a lizard and now, we've got 123 of them."

What kind of problems will the multiple-lizards pose for the Schoenberg family?

Creche Programme

Their local council, Liverpool, has already promised a crash programme on creche facilities, meals-on-wheels, round-the-clock nursing care and an all-expenses paid holiday in Sri Lanka to give the proud mother and father "a complete break" from this appalling nightmare which has been foisted on them by the *Mail on Sunday* in association with medical science.

A Doctor writes

AS A DOCTOR I am often asked "Why do you never win by-elections?"

Well, as yet there is no simple answer to this problem. What happens in cases like these is that the Doctor suffers continually from coming second, or *Tacticalvotus Torieswinagensis* to give it its full medical name.

The symptoms persist for years and the condition may prove fatal.

There is no known cure for this disease.

© *World Copyright A. Doctor Owen.*

Oman contract

Maggie cleared

by Our Political Staff Sir Alan Watneys

MRS THATCHER was today "totally completely, and utterly exonerated of any suggestion of impropriety whatsoever" in connection with the award of the Oman contract to Cementation Ltd.

A special MP's committee considered all the evidence for five minutes before declaring the Prime Minister 100% blameless in every respect.

AMAZING

The Whitewash Commitee was set up under the Chairmanship of Sir Humphrey Whitewash, 82, (East Wapshott, Con.) and other members of the Committee were as follows: Lord Brownose (North Stoddart, Con.), Sir Hugo Thatcher (no relation) (Neasden Super Mare, Con.) and Mrs Sally Opensesame (Lymeswold, Con.)

Let's Gagner D'Argent One More Temps

Lesson Numero Quatre-Vingt-Quatorze:

Dans Le Bookshop

Customer: Bonjour monsieur. . .

Le Bookseller: Bonjour.

Customer: Avec vous quelque chose pour un good laugh dans les vacances?

Le Bookseller: Bien sur, guv. J'ai just le chose pour vous. Take a charcuterie at ceci, matey.

Customer: Oh non! Pas Miles Kington encore!

Le bookseller: Oui, oui c'est tres amusant and cote-splitting je vous assure.

Customer: Parlez de flogging un cheval mort, I ask you.

Le Bookseller: Mais non tous les livres sont completement different. Par example nous avons *Let's Parler Franglais. Let's Parler Franglais Encore, Let's Parler Franglais Un Troisieme Temps, More of the Meme Chose, Le Best de Let's Parler Franglais, Let's Parler Franglais Till We're Bleu in the Face.* . .

Customer: Dites no more! Ce Kington certainement a un sanglant nerve, n'est-ce pas?

Bookseller: Have it your own facon, mon ami. Alors, si Monsieur Kington n'est pas your tasse de tea, how about ce petit number ici?

Customer: Mon dieu! *Le Complete Jokes d'Alan Coren.* Crikey, non! Donnez moi le Kington toute suite!

Bookseller: Merci, squire. Ca sera three ninety-nine!

Customer: Au revoir.

ANYTHING WORTH FIGHTING TWO WORLD WARS FOR MUST BE WORTH FIGHTING A THIRD ONE FOR

It took two world wars before the nations of Europe learnt how to live together in peace.

Today we don't need to settle our difficulties with tanks and guns. We've learned to live side by side in a spirit of harmony and co-operation.

That's not to say that we see eye to eye on everything.

Of course we don't.

You wouldn't expect us to go round kow-towing to a lot of greasy foreigners who can't even speak our language, would you?

Look at the way they've been trying to get us to pay through the nose for their beastly Euro-Budget — just so that a lot of Frog peasants can sit around swilling wine and getting even richer.

Look at the way they've been hi-jacking our meat lorries and turning away our bona-fide tourists just because of the colour of their skins.

They've even started shooting unarmed British football supporters just because they were having a bit of innocent fun turning over a few cars.

Well, we've got news for you Johnny-Euro.

There's only one language you people have ever understood.

We gave it to you in 1914 and again in 1939.

And, by Golly, in the immortal words of Winston Churchill, we're going to give it to you again.

Yes, it's war.

"Mondale is very wonderful human being"
Fraggle's shock claim

by Our San Francisco Staff
Sir Alistair Brunette and Sir Robin Gay

Senator Gareth Fraggle

The Rev. Michael Jackson

SENATOR Garry Fraggle today brought a packed convention hall to its feet, cheering, sobbing and singing negro spirituals as he described Mr Walter Mundane as "my oldest friend and a deeply sincere Christian".

Taking out an onion, Senator Fraggle called Mr Mundane "the only possible choice as the candidate of our great Democratic Party" and confessed that he had secretly always hoped that he himself would not get the nomination.

FRAUD

Earlier the 50,000 delegates to the Convention had wept openly when the Rev. Sammy Davis Jr. had described the Democratic Party as "a great rainbow in the sky made up of all the colours in the spectrum, especially black".

Holding his arms wide to the delegates, the Rev. Jesse James went on "Missah Mundane, mah children, is de angel appointed by de Lawd to lead America into de Promised Land, so make sho y'all go out and help him to beat dat white trash Reagan in November".

GARBAGE

Scarcely had delegates dried their eyes, when they once again burst into paroxysms of sobs at the arrival on stage of Ms Gloria Farrago, who was described by Mr Mundane as "the most very wonderful and real human being it has ever been my privilege to have as a running mate, and what is more she is a woman. Have a nice day".

Next on the stage appeared the new Democrat campaign manager Bert J. Crook, who was described by Rev. Jessie Fraggle as "a deeply committed human being and a very wonderful Churchgoer who has deep convictions, most of them for tax evasion".

HUMBUG

To close the ceremony, as several million balloons bearing the message "YOU'RE THE FRITZ" floated from the ceiling, Senator Edward Jollygood Chappaquiddick led the weeping congregation in a four-hour rendition of "We shall be overcome in November".

The
Book of Begin

1. Now Begin was full of years and waxed old, even as the pomegranate withereth upon the vine. *(Shome mishtake? God.)*.
2. And, lo, Begin looked upon the land of Lebanon and saw how it had been fulfilled even as it had been written.
3. For did not the prophets of old foretell how it should come to pass that the children of Israel should go forth into the land of everyone else, and should lay them waste, even as the locust hath laid waste the cauliflower of Hebron.
4. And Begin called unto him his faithful servant Itzhak Shamir and said unto him "Behold, I am old, and am weary.
5. "For I have performed even as the Lord had ordained. I have gone forth into the land of Lebanon and the land of Golan and the land on the west side of Jordan and there I have smitten the following persons, namely Arabites, Maronites, Phalangites, Druzites, Shi'ites, Stalagmites Marmites, Catamites and other tribes of the gentiles too numerous to mention."
6. Then said Shamir unto him, "Verily, thou hast smitten off more than thou canst chew."
7. But Begin said unto Shamir "Now is the evening of my days and it is time for me to be taken up into heaven like Elijah, and for the Lord to say until me "Well done, my good and faithful servant, for thou hast obeyed my commandments and thou hast improved on them a bit with regard to the smiting."
8. And Begin offered his resignation the first time.
9. But the children of Israel looked upon his offer of resignation and there was great wailing and gnashing of teeth.
10. For they said unto Begin, "Thou hast got us into this mess, with thy smiting, and only thou canst get us out."
11. And Begin hearkeneth to them and said "Verily I say unto you that I shall resign next Tuesday instead."
12. And there was great wailing and building of settlements.
HERE ENDETH THE FIRST BOOK OF BEGIN.
Next week beginneth the Return of Begin.

THE ALTERNATIVE VOICE

Dave Spart, Secretary of the Bermondsey "Coal Not Dole" Support Action Group, talks frankly and fearlessly about the latest moves in the Miners' Dispute.

ONCE again the Capitalist media are indulging in an orgy of sickening hypocrisy condemning the so-called "violence" on the picket line which amounts to no more than totally legitimate and peaceful protest whilst at the same time turning a totally blind eye to the real violence in our society ie the sustained attack on the working classes by Thatcher and her henchmen ie unemployment the across the board cuts in welfare services VAT on working class food ie take-away this is the real violence which the media er (cont p94)

"Oh no! Not again! – I've only just paid my rates!"

FACE THE PRESS

with

Neil Kinnock

ROBERT CARVEL *(for it is he):* Mr Kinnock, since you became leader of the Labour Party, the suggestion has been widely made that you are nothing more than a Welsh windbag. How do you react to that charge?

KINNOCK: Well, you know, boyo, it's all very well for people to go round, look you, making these absurd allegations, these vapid charges, these ridiculous assertions, but you know, look you, when you're in the business of politics like I am, you've got to get used to this cheap, abusive type of remark – no, don't get me wrong, boyo, you're only doing your job, and I appreciate that – and one of the great values of our democratic society is that everyone, no matter of what persuasion or faith or creed, is perfectly entitled to come on the television and make this kind of ridiculous, extravagant and quite preposterous type of suggestion that I am a Welsh windbag, when nothing could be more transparently not the case – no, let me finish, I just want to say that anyone who thinks that I am physically incapable of answering a simple question in less than twenty minutes must need their (contd. p.94).

MASSIVE TORY REVOLT

BACKBENCH PROTEST GROWS

by Our Political Staff
A.N. Watneys

In the blackest week for the government so far, Mrs. Thatcher yesterday faced a massive new threat from inside her own party.

The mood in Westminster last night was ugly. The knives were out. The bovver boys of the Tory right were prowling the corridors thirsting for blood.

CRISIS

Events came to a head when shortly before midnight Tory MP Sir Bufton Tufton put down a shock motion of censure which rocked an already tottering cabinet to its foundations.

Bluntly Sir Bufton spelt out just what many backbenchers feel today about the woman who led them into two election triumphs, but whose reputation now hangs by a shred.

The much-respected Tory stalwart left no one in any doubt as to his feelings: His motion read as follows:

"That this House, whilst fully supporting the actions and record of the Prime Minister in every respect whatsoever, regrets that in some cases the government may be failing to put across its message sufficiently clearly for everyone to realise how utterly wonderful and correct it is. God Save Mrs. Thatcher."

Sir Bufton is 81.

Jagger at 80

by Peter Yobboe

Mr. Yobboe, who was a founder member of the popular singing group **Who He?**, *is now an editorial director of the distinguished publishing house Fabber and Fabber.*

FEW WHO were privileged to witness the recent "charity gig" performed by Sir Michael Jagger at Blenheim Palace would immediately have thought that they were in the presence of a man of 80 – such is the extraordinary animal magnetism of this now-legendary artist. It is nearly a century since Sir Michael first electrified his young audiences of the 'sixties with such lyrics as "*I Wanna Jerk Off the Whole Bloody World.*" Later of course his preoccupations took a more metaphysical turn, as in his celebrated Satanic invocation of 1968 "*Hullo Mr. Freakout Devil Man.*"

Today with his rolled umbrella, pinstripe suits and copy of the *Financial Times* casually dropped on the backseat of his Rolls Royce, Sir Michael at first sight seems a very conventional figure. His talk is of the Test Match score, the ups-and-downs of the stock market and the problems he experiences in finding reliable domestic staff. But see him stripped to the waist, dressed in nothing but a glittering leather jock-strap, his false teeth pulsating in the flashing strobe lights, as we feel ourselves at one in the presence of one of the greatest

(cont. p. 94).

"Mrs Thatcher sank defenceless Labour Party"

– MP's shock claim

by Our Defence Correspondent Tam O'Ranter

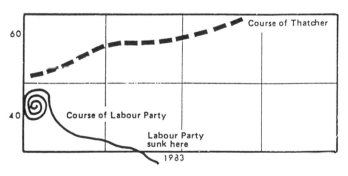

Course of Thatcher

60

Course of Labour Party

40

Labour Party sunk here

1983

In the summer campaign of 1983, Mrs Thatcher deliberately and without provocation sank the Labour Party, an MP claimed today.

Mr Tam Daloony, 73, told journalists that he had "definite proof" that the Labour Party posed no threat whatever to Mrs Thatcher.

GAUCHO MARX

"It was an old coaster" he said

"which at the time of the incident was drifting around trying to work out where it was."

Mr Daloony said the sinking was a criminal act designed solely to increase Mrs Thatcher's prestige.

"All hands were lost" he said "and the Skipper, Vice Admiral Dozi Worzelio, went down with the ship and was never seen again."

Mr Daloony is 89.

"And that, m'lud, concludes the case for the prosecution"

"Typical! You wait ages for Godot, then three come at once!"

★ WHITE ★ HOUSE '84

★ ★ ★ ★ ★ ★ ★

An Extended All-Night Satellite-Link Election Special with David Dimbleby, Sir Alastair Brunette, John Timpson, Frank Bough, Selina Scott, Sir Peter Jaybotham, Roald Rat, Cannon and Ball, with additional contributions from Sir Sandwell Gall in Afghanistan, Mark Tully in Delhi, Mark Delhi in Tully and Tim Sebastian in Uganda.

DIMBLEBORE *(for it is he):*
CAPTIONED 'LIVE FROM WASHINGTON'.

Good evening and welcome to our seven-hour US Election Special. For the next eight hours we shall be bringing you live coverage of the 1984 race for the White House, as the results come in all through the 50 States making up the USA.

(Walks over to large wall-map showing States with flashing lights)

DIMBLEBORE: Make no mistake, although things seem to have been going President Reagan's way, the result of his gripping 42nd race for the Presidency of the world's most powerful nation is by no means a forgone conclusion....

CAPTION COMES UP:
'REAGAN ELECTED'.

....If the polls are to be believed, President Reagan looks like a winner. But the pollsters have been proved wrong before....

CAPTION: 'MONDALE CONCEDES DEFEAT'.

....Is it possible that Walter Mondale could be about to pull off the biggest shock upset since President Watneys defeated Senator Hiram Wheatcroft in 1922?

CAPTION: 'NO'.

(Boring man with bow-tie and pipe appears on satellite link)
CAPTION: 'LIVE FROM MILWAUKEE, KARL J. PIPESUCKER'.

DIMBLEBORE: Prof. Pipesucker, you have been writing about American elections for over 70 years. Are we to believe the polls, or can we look forward tonight to a tremendous surprise?

CAPTION: 'I SAID NO'.

PIPESUCKER: Well of course we've all been recalling in recent days the unforgettable election turn-around of 1948, when, if you remember, the American people went to bed believing that Governor Dewey had won a landslide over the incumbent President Harry Truman, who of course was....

DIMBLEBORE: I'm sorry Professor, I must interrupt you there because we are going over live to Selina Scott-Joplin in the little New Hampshire town of Hicksville, which has always traditionally been known as the barometer of

America....I believe that something is happening over there in Hicksville — Selina?

SCOTT-JOPLIN *(Standing outside snowswept Clapboard House in pitch darkness — reading from clapboard):* "The little town of Hicksville has long been traditionally known as the barometer of America...."
CAPTION: 'GET ON WITH IT'.
(Man in lumber-jacket eating hamburger and drinking Budweiser wanders into shot)

SCOTT: Excuse me, Sir, as a typical middle-American, may I ask you how you cast your vote today?
CAPTION: 'QUEEN SENDS MESSAGE OF CONGRATULATION TO REAGAN'.

MAN *(ARNOLD B. KOESTLER, for it is he):* Howdy, ma'am. They do say as how us folks here in Hicksville are kinda like a barometer for the whole of these here United States. God bless America. Thank you ma'am. Have a nice day.

SCOTT: Well, we'll be giving you the verdict of the seven voters here in Hicksville just as soon as they've completed the count. Meanwhile it's back to you, David, in Washington.

DIMBLEBORE: Well here the first indications are that President Reagan has begun to establish something of a lead, but I must emphasise that it is very early days yet and it would be premature to

make any predictions about the final outcome on the basis of the few scattered results we have so far got in.
CAPTION: 'REAGAN NAMES CABINET'.

DIMBLEBORE: Meanwhile we have here in the studio a panel of extremely distinguished bores who are going to drone on for the next few hours, including Prof. Arthur Schlesinger Jr., formerly Special Policy Affairs Director to President Kennedy....
(Shot of boring man with bow-tie)
....Dr. Donald Slazenger, formerly Special Advisor on Foreign Affairs to President Johnson....
(Shot of second boring man with bow-tie)
....and Mr Harry J. Lozenger, formerly Policy Director of the Congressional Political Affairs Unit.
(Shot of third boring man with bow-tie)
CAPTION: 'MONDALE QUITS POLITICS'.

DIMBLEBORE: Might I begin by asking you all whether you think President Reagan is likely to be given the second term he is after, or are we in for a big surprise?
CAPTION: 'OF COURSE NOT'.

J.D. SALINGER: Well, of course, the implications of your question are essentially twofold. Might I begin by rephrasing your....

DIMBLEBORE: Professor, I'm afraid I'll have to

break in there, as we are going over live to the traditional Democratic heartland of Louisiana, a state which our computer tells us Mr.Mondale *has* to win if he is to upset the pollsters.

BRIAN REDHEAD: Good evening, Alastair. I am standing here in the little cotton-picking community of Belmooney, on the banks of the Mississippi, where I am trying to feel the pulse of this very old black person here — one of the greatest exponents of the 12-string banjo this country has even produced, Blind Lemon Shandy Levine.

LEVINE *(Rocking slowly in chair and strumming tunelessly on banjo):* Why, suh, I wuz hopin' to cast mah vote for dat President Roosevelt, who done freed all us slaves back in de bad ole days, when ah spied this li'l ol' groun-hog a-scratchin' and a-scroungin' 'roun' de ol' water melon patch, an' ah says to mahself, Lemon Shandy, ah says, de Laud be praised, why, dis here li'l ol' groun' hog is sho' goin' to end up on mah dinner plate with red beans and rice, or mah name isn't Blind Lemon Shandy Levine, suh.

ALISTAIR COOKE: I was playing a round of golf with my old friend President Lincoln last week and he *(cont. p.94)*

★ ★

Sir JONAH JUNOR
CURRENT EVENTS

Every week a well-known taxi driver is asked to comment on an issue of current interest:
This week:
The Brighton Bomb

Eddie Mixer
(Cab No. 41111)

L IKE EVERYONE else I was shocked and horrified by the tragic death of Mrs Gandhi.

I have been second to no-one in my admiration of this fine and courageous woman.

But didn't one thing strike you as odd?

In all the fulsome tributes there was not a single mention of her husband, Mr Gandhi.

I am not suggesting for a moment that Indira married him for his name and then quietly got rid of him when he was of no more use to her.

But perhaps young Rajiv should make it one of his first tasks to clear the air once and for all about his father's mysterious disappearance.

A BUSY man, Mr Kinnock, isn't he? He tells his old friend Arthur Scargill that he will be unable to speak at any of the Miners' Rallies.

His excuse: prior engagements on every single one of the twenty three dates suggested.

No doubt Mr Kinnock is telling the truth on this occasion.

But I feel sure that Glenys Kinnock, along with all the rest of us, would like to know just exactly where he will be on all these dates.

Shouldn't he clear the air and tell us precisely what his mysterious "engagements" involve?

KING ARTHUR'S latest edict to his followers orders them to flush their toilets every night on the dot of 6pm.

The idea, he tells us, is to put an intolerable strain on the electric sewage pumps in the hope that they will be brought to a standstill.

I am only too happy to oblige – on one condition. That Mr Sewage himself first climbs into the bowl.

This way, Arthur. And don't forget to wipe your feet.

CAPT. "BOB" Maxwell had a narrow escape when he flew out to Ethiopia on his "mercy mission".

He was lucky to get home safe and sound, in my opinion.

I am told that in some parts of Africa they have slightly different dietary habits to those of the grain-loving Ethiopians.

Wouldn't it have been terrible if the ample figure of Captain Bob had ended up in the pot?

I reckon 'ooever did that there's only one fing to do wiv 'im and that's string the bleeder up by 'is bloody neck. That's the only language those people understand. Bloody animals that's all they are. Bastards. D'you want to known what I fink they should do wiv the Micks? I fink they should drop the bomb on Belfast. That'd shut them up, wouldn't it guv?

I 'ad that Terry Wogan in the back of the cab once.

Next Week: Vic Smut.

"Rapists, child-molesters OK; what I can't tolerate are transvestites"

POUND REACHES PARITY WITH PENNY

Lawson says "WE'RE RIGHT ON COURSE"

AS THE pound soared to a new low of 0.993p yesterday, Mr Nigel Lawson lashed out at his critics by explaining that what he called "this technical re-adjustment in the value of sterling" was due to a whole range of factors outside the government's control.

"In particular" he claimed "there is an obvious correlation between the sharp drop in the value of the pound and the cold spell we have been having recently."

"This sort of factor is obviously something that we can none of us predict, but it should not shake anyone's faith in the underlying value of the pound."

Sterling. You Were Wonderful

"The pound in your suitcase" he gibbered on, "is still worth almost as much as it was five minutes ago, and you must all agree, gentlemen, that it really has been jolly cold."

"In fact" Mr Lawson concluded, "considering the severity of the weather conditions, it is little short of a miracle that the pound is worth anything at all. it is a clear vote of confidence in the policies of this government."

That historic Hong Kong Agreement in full

AN Historic Agreement Reached Between Her Britannic Majesty's Government and the People's Republic of China in This Year of the Rat 1984.

1.

IN accordance with the solemn and binding agreement dated 1 July 1887 the People's Republic of China now requests and demands that the Island of Hong Kong and surrounding territories should be returned on 1 January 1997 double-quick.

2.

SIR Geoffrey Howe agrees to the above.

G. HOWE H.M.G.,   HOW GEE P.R.C.

Signed,

Chinese acclaim Howe's brilliant diplomacy

by Our Man in Peking
Hoo Hee

Last night Chinese ruling circles were full of praise for the "outstanding gifts" of Britain's tough negotiator Sir Geoffrey Howe.

"Whatever we demanded" said one senior Chinese official, "Sir Geoffrey, with consummate skill and patience, agreed to at once.

"Had it not been for Sir Geoffrey" the Peking source continued, "these negotiations could well have been very difficult for us. As it was, thanks to the superb spinelessnes of your Sir Geoffrey, it was all over in a couple of minutes."

Sir Geoffrey Howe is 76.

On Other Pages:
Howe Gets Tough With Argies...p. 74.
Howe Tells Madrid – "Hands Off Our Gib"...p. 8.
"Keep Out Of Ulster" – Howe Warns Dublin ...p. 10.

Old Bores Corner

**Me and My Books
by BERNARD LEVIN**

Ever since I was two I have been a voracious reader. Here are some of the books which I have read:

*Moby Dick, Great Expectations, A La Recherche du Temps Perdu, Robinson Crusoe, Huckleberry Finn, Mansfield Park, War and Peace, Ivor the Engine Goes on Holiday (**Shome Mishake Surely?**)* *(Contd. p. 94).*

"Class of '68, am I right?"

DAILY Mirror

Saturday, July 14, 1984   FORWARD WITH BRITAIN   ★   ·17p.

JANE TAKES ALL HER CLOTHES OFF!

ELVIS IS TOP OF THE POPS!

Daily Mirror
YES - IT'S NEW MIRROR BINGO!

● THREE Great Moments in the Mirror's History: and this is the greatest ever!

FORWARD WITH MAXWELL!

AT LAST I've done it. I own a National Newspaper! Ever since I was a small boy I have wanted to become a big-shot in Fleet Street. And now I am. What is more I am proud to be the proprietor of such an integral part of the British way of life.

Maxwell

Let me make one thing absolutely clear. I am not a power crazed multi-millionaire who wants to own a national newspaper. Rest assured, my aim is for the Daily Maxwell to be an independent voice speaking out on behalf of the underprivileged, drawing attention to injustice and forging a new Britain and er...that sort of thing...

Robert Maxwell

The Maxwell has always been a supporter of the Labour Party. From its very beginnings it has spoken out on

Robert Maxwell (owner)

by ROBERT MAXWELL
Publisher of The Daily Maxwell

behalf of the underprivileged, drawing attention to injustice and forging a new... etc...

That is why my slogan says it all: Forward with Maxwell!

On other pages

WHY MAGGIE IS RIGHT   Page 5

Mirror Comment
WHY PRISON IS TOO GOOD FOR SCARGILL   Page 7

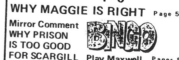

Play Maxwell   Pages 8, 9, 10
Housey-Housey

The Owl and the Pussy Cat Edward Lear (1822-1894)

The owl and the Pussy Cat
went to sea
In a beautiful pea-green Boat.
Da dum de dum plenty of
honey,
Fill in the next bit could you,
old boy.

I bet most people know this one. They bloody well ought to do.

Some people say it's just a nonsense poem. But there's quite a lot of evidence to suggest that Edward Lear was homo-sexually involved with Alfred Lord Tennyson and that the poem is deeply obscene.

Can I have my money please? K.A.

Famine horror latest

Maxwell flies in

by Our Man in Ethiopia Alan Korem

A beaming, ebullient Cardinal Robert Maxwell, leader of Britain's four million *Mirror*-readers, today flew in to the capital of famine-torn Ethiopia to distribute millions of free bingo cards to the starving people of this unhappy land.

Plainly shaken by his plane ride, the Captain told his startled Ethiopian hosts "This is your lucky day – do you realise that I could soon be making one of you a Bingo Millionaire."

The Captain was then taken to see for himself the huge numbers of massed Soviet tanks which have been gathered together to ferry Western grain to the starving millions.

RUNNING DERGS

After presenting his hosts with a signed copy of *The Complete Speeches of President Cherenko*, Captain Maxwell left for a 15-course fact-finding dinner at the Addis Ababa People's Revolutionary Hilton Hotel.

Time to come out of the close...

Hundreds of Bishops waste their lives sitting around in cathedrals taking services – when they could be international celebrities.

If you're a Bishop who feels he's missing out on the new Bishop Boom then it could be time to get your act together.

Gnome Mitre-Media Services now offer you a full range of media events to suit your personality.

What's more, we can supply any amount of controversial issues which you can sound off about.

Nuclear War. The Miners Strike. The Bomb. Arthur Scargill – these are only a handful of the headline-grabbing topics which will guarantee you instant nationwide media coverage.

Don't just hang around the cloisters like a dozy old monk. Get controversial. Get out of your gaiters – get into the news.

For further details write to: Gnome Mitre-Media Services.

Branches in: Barchester, Abu-Dhabi, Neasden.

Lines on the Christening of Prince Harry
and the failure of
HRH Princess Anne to attend the ceremony

by the new Poet Laureate
TED WHOHEGHS

Under Balbooley crag
In an eddy of whirlpools
Flows

The Crow.
Black clouds crack
With thunder as
Old milk bottles
Bob, fizz, thunder
Under
The Crow

Scargill Moor
Mist-draped
Sheep wet, old trousers
Left to rot
And the Kerridge
Rising from beneath
Dark dungeons
Filled with white bones
Of dead
Crows
Surges down the side
Of Morecambe Fell
Dripping blood
From the shaggy pores
Of the dead sheep
Eddies gurgling over
Jags of polished bones

Detergent bottles
Twisting and writhing past
Rusty bedspreads
Strewn like giant
Crows

On old half-covered
Mouldy turnips
The stench of dying
Bleeding laughing (shome mishtake?)
Rabbits hits the
Nostril like shrapnel
The stomach churns
Like the waters of
Gowrie Bilgarth
In the rainy season
When the dead fish
Drift half silver
Half green like
Crows
Down down down
Towards the Sunlit
Pool beneath Scar Mooly
Where the green slime
Coagulates in a film
Of brackish brown garbage
Will this do?

Ted W.

Ronald Reagan's Ireland

Well, Bejasus! (Isn't that what the Irish say?)

There's certainly no place like Ireland. For a start it's always raining.

It's pretty depressing, really. Rundown. Dull. No wonder they all take to drink.

You can certainly see why my ancestors got the hell out of the place.

Still a man's gotta do what a man's gotta do.

And what I've gotta do is get the Irish vote when I run for President again.

Sure and begorrah. (*Takes out onion*) when I see the mountains of Ballyporeen and the oysters of Dublin's Fair City I think to myself how much longer have I got to stay in this Godforsaken dump?

The most interesting people go to Ireland

D·Day recalled

An old soldier looks back

Recluse lashes out

by Sir Herbert Gussett

THOSE of us who were privileged to live through that historic day 40 years ago when the evil forces of Nazi barbarism were at last swept into the sea, can only echo the immortal words of the Bard:

"We few, who were living at that hour
On this sceptr'd isle, set in a silver sea
Once more unto the beach dear friends
And so to bed." (Please check the wording. H.G.)

I shall never forget that day, as long as I can remember it. For months we had thought of little else. The narrow lanes of southern England were filled with our gum-chewing friends from "across the herring pond", with their jeeps and pictures of Betty Grable.

Then suddenly, the day dawned. The skies were filled with thousands of little ships making their way across the Channel. It was unforgettable.

How can I possibly convey to the young people of today with their so-called "punk" haircuts and clutching their Sony Walkmen, what it was like to be actually there on what has become known so appropriately as "the longest day"?

It will be indelibly etched in my memory as long as I live, the cacophony of noise and smoke, the sickening stench as I arrived on that June morning in the saloon bar of the Lamb and Flag — just in time to hear the imperishable voice of Mr. Alvar Liddell announcing from the wireless set on the bar the historic news:

"Allied troops based somewhere in Southern England today landed somewhere in Northern France. Further details will be made available in 1974 under the 30-year rule."

Train arrives shock

by *Our British Rail Correspondent* **A.** *Wayday*

THOUSANDS of rail passengers yesterday gasped with disbelief when a train arrived safely at a London terminus.

Said one uninjured passenger Mrs Enid Wheatcroft, 47, "It was amazing. As the train approached, we suddenly realised that it was not going to burst into flames, or fall off the rails or strike any obstacle. Everybody kept calm, and went on reading the Daily Telegraph, while the train drew quietly into the platform".

A British Rail spokesman said later that a full enquiry was to be held into "all the circumstances surrounding the safe arrival of the train".

Sir James Savile, MBE, is 86.

"You and I have the ideal relationship"

Help to Save One of Europe's Most Glorious Treasures.

The Queen Mother in peril appeal

For centuries Her Majesty the Queen Mother, known as 'La Serenissima'', has been held in affection by countless millions.

With her radiant handbag and smiling hat the Queen Mother has attracted visitors from all over the world.

But now experts who have examined her foundations believe that she may well be in danger of sinking beneath a tidal wave of gin and tonic, causing decay and subsidence.

Send all donations to the Queen Mother in Peril. *Patrons:* John Julius Norwich, the Late Lord Clark, Norman St. John Stevas *(Telegrams and Cables: OLDQUEEN).*

TUESDAY PAGE

Those Rock–on Royals

Who are they? The new generation of the Royal Family, the young go-ahead swingers who are giving a new look to that stuffy old Regal Image?
by **Bevis Hillier** and **Sir Even Sillier**

Lady Jane Sloane

Lady Caroline Windsor-Davis

She could be any young 'raver' walking down the Kings Road in her trendy gear and faded denim jeans.

But no. She is Lady Sarah Bufton Sprargs, fourteenth in line to the throne of England.

Lady Zara is typical of the new-look Royal Family of today. One minute she could be sharing a hamburger with her art student friends, the next attending a Royal Banquet side by side with the Queen Mother.

Lady Windsor-Simpson is currently working on a new film project with her cousin Lord Letchfield and she will resume her History of Art studies at the Guggenheim Institute, Venice, in the autumn.

Viscount Carnaby

David Ormsby Prattface Gore-Booth, first Viscount Carnaby, is only nineteen but he has already carved a name for himself in the stripped pine table that he recently "knocked up" for the new chic Chelsea dining spot Eatz 'n' Drinkz. (He thought of the name himself!)

Viscount Burnaby did a two-month course in table design at the prestigious institut de Dessin de La Table in Paris before taking up photography under his father Lord Letchfield.

Last year he had a photograph of himself published in the *Tatler* and this year he is hoping to get one into *Harpers Queen*.

Lady Mary Rose Sandringham is only nineteen yet already she has established herself in the public eye as what the Royal Family are looking like in the Eighties: casual, smart – and with a touch of zany humour.

Lady Godiva once swam top-less on a beach in the South of France. The next week she was walking side by side with the Queen Mother in Westminster Abbey.

In her faded denim jacket and sunglasses from Dalucci's in Fulham Road Lady Ludmilla could easily be mistaken for her close friend Lady Cynthia Marmalade Paradine.

Lady Belinda, like many members of the Royal Family is passionately interested in the world of Arts. At present she works one morning a week at Kolnargis's Gallery in New Bond Street where she makes coffee and phone-calls to her friends.
(That's enough new-look Royals. Ed.)

THE KREMLIN'S NEW BROOM

The emergence of MR. MIKHAIL GORBLIMOV as the new leader of the Soviet Union seems likely to herald a major breakthrough in East-West relations. Mr. Gorblimov is an entirely new type of figure in the history of Soviet politics. In contrast to his predecessors, Mr. Gorblimov is astonishingly youthful. He is the first Soviet leader not to be shackled by memories of the Revolution and the Stalinist era. In comparison with Mr. Chernenko, Mr. Gorblimov is like a breath of spring after a long, hard Siberian winter. He is approachable.....smiles easily..... liberal outlook.....sense of humour.....attractive wife..... Parisian suits.....lover of Western jazz.....gourmet.....conoisseur of fine wines.....finds Karl Marx "intensely boring".

Nevertheless it would be a mistake to exaggerate the extent of Mr. Gorblimov's heterodoxy. Behind his apparent air of relaxed good humour, his disarming smile and his elegant Savile Row suits, Mr. Gremlin conceals a ruthlessly shrewd mind, clamped fast in the rigorous confines of the traditional Marxist-Leninist mould.... years of slavish obedience to Party hierarchy.....remorseless ambition.....hard-hearted........ gimlet eyes.....frumpy wife..... admirer of Stalin. There can be little doubt that the arrival of Mr. Gorblimov heralds a new phase of hard nosed confrontation in East-West affairs, a veritable new ice age after the brief, hopeful spring of Mr. Chernenko.

A Doctor writes

Wogan

AS A doctor I am often asked "Is Terry Wogan bad for you?" The short answer is that, taken once a week, Terry Wogan or *Wogan Borus ubiquitus* to give its full medical name, is not particularly harmful. However, we doctors know very little about the effects of taking it more frequently. Three times a week may well prove a health hazard and patients are advised to limit their dosage.

If you are worried about Wogan you should consult professional medical advice at once.

"Bad news, I'm afraid. The Israelites have developed a new range of musical instruments that destroy walls but leave people standing. . ."

© 'A Doctor'

"I've had this great mediocre idea for a book"

"You patronising bastard!"

"See what I mean Achmed, it's not the deterrent it used to be"

"The new manager is quite a 'go-getter' isn't he?"

Bishop reaffirms faith in traditional story

by Our Religious Correspondent Don Selwyn-Stupitt

THE controversial Bishop of Durham today reaffirmed his belief in the "literal truth" of the famous story of the boy who was unable to go to school because he had no shoes.

Said the Bishop "Christians believe that the boy without shoes who was unable to go to school does indeed exist as a historical person."

GOSPEL TRUTH

Previously on a television programme the Bishop had given the impression that it was not necessary for Christians to accept the boy with no shoes as "a historical fact".

"To many" he said, "the idea of the boy with no shoes is a source of inspiration and hope in a very real sense, regardless of whether or not he actually existed.

"To my mind one does not have to accept the literal truth of the story to be a committed Christian."

VOLTE FARCE

Now however the Bishop says he "believes passionately" in the story not "as myth" but "as fact".

"This boy, whose name escapes me" he said yesterday "dwells amongst us. And what is more there are thousands of boys like him without clothes or food who are forced to become chimney sweeps and work in the cotton mills to avoid the work-house."

Bishop Jenkins is 103.

Every week a well-known taxi-driver is asked to comment on an issue of topical importance. This week:

The Miners Strike

by Fred Gozzer
(Cab No. 77731)

That Scargill I mean if I 'ad my way 'e'd be swingin' from a rope. That bloke before 'im that Joe Gormley I 'ad a lot of time for 'im but Arfur Scargill and his thugs I mean why don't they go back to Russia if that's what they want? I'm not sayin' MacGregor is any better mind you. At 'is age 'e should be in a bath chair not running a major industry. There's only one thing for it for my money and that's to call in the army and sort out those pickets once and for all. I 'ad that Robert Maxwell in the back of the cab once.

Next week: Reg Blimey

Chess Problem
with "Old Bore"

Old Bore writes: This very long drawn out game looked headed for a certain stalemate, until a surprise intervention by the Red Bishop, attacking the old King, threw spectators into a frenzy of boredom. Can you see how the game is going to end?

Answer: page 94.

Scargill (Red)

MacGregor (White)

IN AT THE
DEEP
END

Every week a complete novice is given a chance to try his hand at something he has never done before and for which he has no natural abilities.

THIS WEEK: **David Jenkins** has a go at being **BISHOP OF DURHAM.**

Shot of sleepy cathedral close with Barchester-style men sitting in the sun reading the Church Times.

JENKINS (*voice over*): I'd always thought that being a Bishop involved quite a lot of hard work. After all, the Bishop is where the buck stops. Parishioners and clergy look up to him for guidance. What better way for me to learn how to be a Bishop than to go right to the very top.

Shot of Runcieballs in ceremonial silver vestments sitting in armchair while his wife lies sprawled on top of the grand piano.

RUNCIEBALLS: An awful lot of people, you know, in a very real sense still expect the Bishops to uphold the traditional teachings of the Christian Church. But nowadays our job is just as much, if not more so, to illuminate the many social, political and economic issues that confront present day society – and that means the media.

Cut to shot of Runcie in Westminster Abbey rehearsing the next coronation.

JENKINS: All very well for him, but I only had a few days before my big test – a full scale enthronement in York Minster in front of TV cameras and millions of people. No wonder I went to seek the advice of the Church's top TV performer – Don Stupitt.

STUPITT (*sitting in make-up room being powdered*): If you're going to go on to religious programmes, ducky, for heaven's sake don't talk about God. That's a real turn-off nowadays. Or if you are going to bring Jesus and all that biblical bit, try and relate it to the miners' strike or something topical. But whatever you do don't take it literally, or they'll never have you back on.

Shot of Jenkins being dressed in Bishop's Robe. He puts on mitre and looks in mirror nervously.

JENKINS: So here it is, my big day. All I have to do is to remember my lines and look as if I believe in it all.

Shot of Jenkins in pulpit reading sermon.

JENKINS: . . . .and I'm sure in my heart of hearts that if the Son of that Nazarene carpenter were alive today He would doubtless be on the picket line shoulder to shoulder with Mr Scargill. And now we sing our final hymn "We Shall Overcome".

Shot of Bishops drinking sherry in TV hospitality room.

RUNCIE: I thought you did very well indeed, Geoffrey, especially for a first timer.

STUPITT: A lot of promise I think. I liked your hatchet job on the Resurrection.

Shot of York Minister in flames.

JENKINS: Oh, God, it looks as if I made a bit of a balls of it after all. . . .

NEXT WEEK: John Selwyn Gummer trying to be Chairman of the Conservative Party.

Let's make it a Happy Christmas (and a confident New Year) in the pit villages.

As Christmas approaches *(takes out onion)* it becomes increasingly difficult for striking miners to afford even the bare essentials to make their life tolerable.

We the undersigned say the miners have a right to enjoy their Christmas just like anyone else.

This is an urgent appeal for a huge bonus for striking miners and their pickets. A little money goes a long way.

£2 will buy a small brick to throw at the police.

£3 a slightly larger brick.

£10 will buy a good quality baseball bat.

£20 will buy a reinforced steel spike.

£100 will buy a concrete pillar weighing well over half a ton.

Please send off your donation now.

This appeal is made by:
Sir Larold O'Ladlier
Rolph Stoddy
Dave Spart
Paul Spart
Rt. Hon Michael Spart
Dame Carmen Virago
The late Spigismond Topes
Rev J.C. Flannel

●
Bel Grano
Geo Melly
Pete Yobbo (Managing Director Fabber and Fabber)
The Incredible Exploding Galaxy (except for Kevin Nobbis)
Tom Caschler
Hermione Dreadful (The Book Programme)

●
Sir Solomon Rushton
Rev Don Stupitt
Colin Wellargs (Chariots of Fire)
Sir Kenneth Leninspart
Dennis Healey *(Shurley shome mishtake?)*
Jim Ongar
Harriet Harperson
A lot of dreadful sixties actresses

(That's enough names, Ed.)

To Miners Families Christmas Appeal
c/o 14 Whittlesley Street, London SE1 8SL.

I/We enclose a donation of £   for the Miners Families Christmas Appeal (Cheque/PO made out to 'Miners Families Christmas Appeal').
To save costs, no receipt will be sent unless requested. (Tick below)
Please send receipt ☐

NAME

ADDRESS

             Postcode

ORGANISATION (if any)

TV

Serious music. Shifty looking man appears in dimly lit studio.

FRED EMERY (*for it is he*): Good evening. Tonight we have a special filmed report on the forthcoming elections in Rumbabwe.

Film shows agreeable luxury villa complete with swimming pool, Rolls Royces and armed guards waving kalashnikovs.

INTERVIEWER: Mr Ebagum, as we sit here in the peaceful surroundings of your Presidential palace, it is hard to imagine that only a few miles away your troops are arresting thousands of people because they refuse to vote for you in these elections. Is this an entirely democratic way of going about things?

EBAGUM: You are only puttin' dis question because you fail to understand de word democracy in de African sense.

INTERVIEWER: But are you going to put these people on trial according to the due process of law?

EBAGUM: You are only puttin' dis question because you fail to understand de word law in de African sense. As you are fully aware, de whole business of bringin' people on trial, and gettin' together all de evidence that is necessary to prove dem guilty is a very complicated procedure, especially when dey are totally innocent.

INTERVIEWER: So your ultimate aim is to turn Rumbabwe into a one-party state by destroying all opposition?

EBAGUM (*laughing*): But of course – de African looks at things in a very different way from us Westerners. In de new Rumbabwe we are one great big happy family, and anyone who does not want to join in dis great big happy family is quite at liberty to jump into the mass grave anytime he pleases.

Back to studio.

FRED EMERY: That report from Rumbabwe was by one of my colleagues. Next week I shall be introducing another *Panorama* special report on the question "Why am I being paid a fortune every week just to read a few lines from the autocue introducing a film by one of my colleagues?" Until then, good night.

Serious music.

Ebagum Protest shock

The following protest against the above interview has been received from the Rt. Hon Robert Ebagum, President-for-Life of the People's Democratic One-Party, One-Tribe, One-Man Republic of Mugabwe.

Dear Sir,

I am readin' wid total disgust de remarks I am shown makin' in your so-called Panorama film. I am sayin' to you that dis interview wid myself is showin' that you are totally misunderstandin' de African way of killing people and throwin' them into de mass grave, which is a perfectly acceptable and age-old way of holdin' de free and fair elections.

I would only conclude by warnin' you dat if you show any more films of myself makin' dese highly damagin' remarks and telling de barefaced lies, I am sendin' around de lads from de notorious North Korean-trained 5th Brigade to assist you in de process of seein' my point of view.

Cure found for Parkinson's Disease?

A Doctor writes

IT NOW seems that a miracle cure may be in sight for one of the most crippling diseases known to politicians — Parkinson's Disease (or *Torychairman Lovechildensis* as we doctors call it).

For a long time, it was thought, Parkinson's Disease was incurable.

But recent work by a Grantham-born chemist may well have come up with a remedy.

Her method is simple.

The patient waits for nine months or so, until everyone else has cocked it up, and is then reinstated and hailed as the saviour of the party.

There are apparently no bit-on-the-side effects.

Miss Sarah Keays is 32.

Heath–
My alternative strategy for Britain
– In full

YOUR DINNER HAS GONE TO ETHIOPIA

1. Sack that women, at once.
2. Reinstate my goodself as Prime Minister.
3. That's it, with regard to this one.

TEN YEARS–AND WHAT A DIFFERENCE !!

● 10 years ago Mrs Margaret Thatcher became leader of the Conservative Party. World famous beauty expert Glenda Slag looks at the changes that life at the top has brought to the style of this extraordinary woman.

IN 1975, the pound was worth over 2 dollars, unemployment was below 2 million and Britain voted to stay in the Common Market. The country was in crisis and onto the stage stepped a grocer's girl from Grantham. For Margaret Hilda Thatcher it was a daunting challenge but one which she was fully prepared to embrace.

She was to become one of the most successful politicians of all time, but ten years ago she was still looking like a suburban housewife running a bring-and-buy stall. A decade of power was to change all that. No-one then would have described her as being "a really fabulous bird" as one of her colleagues did recently. Nor would the French Prime Minister, Francois Nargs, have commented as he did last week "Zut alors! I'd give my right arm to get my legover zat tasty tomato I tell you!"

With each succeeding year Margaret Thatcher's transformation has been little short of miraculous. It is as if Power has waved its magic wand and worked its spell on every aspect of her appearance. Her hair, her teeth, her eyes, her body have been remoulded into a vision of ecstatic sexuality. Her wardrobe, too, has become less formal, more relaxed as she has learnt to manage her twin roles as statesman and *femme fatale*. Out go the prim hats and demure two-piece outfits of yesteryear. Now she steps into the limelight in the designer styles of the moment: Bertocelli, Carudo, Saatchi... Her accessories come from Cartier not Marks and Spencers, and her silk lingerie is hand-made by the best that Paris has to offer.

No woman in the world excites the same passions when she walks into a room. No man can resist. Ten years ago she was merely another woman. Today she is a goddess. *(That's enough of this rubbish. Ed.)*

THEN

Twee, prim and dull. Not yet touched by the power of high office. Even her voice sounded middle-class.

NOW

Bewitching, beautiful and confidently sensual. Sexual and political power combine to create the perfect woman. Cor!

HOUSE OF COMMONS
OFFICIAL REPORT

PARLIAMENTARY DEBATES

(HANSARD)

Prime Minister's Questions.

2.46 pm

Mr. Neil Kinnock (Flanelly, Lab.): Would the Rt. Hon. Lady, the Prime Minister, like to admit to the House that she was personally responsible for taking the decision to try to put Mr. Ponting behind bars, and would she further like to admit that she has now been caught out in a persistent, sustained and totally persistent attempt seriously to mislead the House ever since 4 May 1982? *[Labour cheers]*

Mrs. Margaret Thatcher (Complete, Con.): How dare the Rt. Hon. Member, the Leader of the Opposition, talk to me like that. *[Conservative cheers]* All I can say in reply to the Rt. Hon. Member is that when the decision to prosecute Mr. Ponting was taken, I was on holiday. I think that completely answers the points he has raised. *[Conservative cheers]*

Mr. Neil Kinnock: Perhaps then the Rt. Hon. Lady would like to enlighten the House as to who was responsible for this deplorable, vengeful and totally deplorable decision? Is she suggesting that it was Sir Michael Havers alone? *[Labour cheers and cries of 'Resign']*

Sir Michael Havers (Molesworth, Con.): If I may just reply personally to that disgraceful allegation, Mr. Speaker, I would like to point out quite categorically to the House that I was also on holiday at the time. *[Conservative groans]*

Mr. Neil Kinnock: Are we then to assume, Mr. Speaker, that the person responsible for taking this decision was the Secretary of State for Defence?

Mr. Speaker: I am afraid the Rt. Hon. Member you refer to is unable to answer that point personally because he is on holiday. *[Labour cries of 'Shame', 'Heseltine out', 'What about the miners?' etc.]*

Mr. Neil Kinnock: Now I've heard everything. I suppose the next lie the Rt. Hon. Lady will be trying to get us all to swallow is that she was on holiday when the decision was taken to sink the Belgrano?

Mrs. Margaret Thatcher: You horrible little Welsh creep! Of course I was on holiday when this deeply distressing incident took place, and I am sure the whole House will join with me in agreeing that, as Prime Minister, it would be quite, quite wrong for me ever to interfere in the running of the country. *[Conservative cries of 'Hear, hear', 'Shame', 'Withdraw', 'Resign', 'We were all on holiday too']*

Mr. Neil Kinnock: I have to say frankly, categorically and quite frankly, that I do not believe a single word that the Rt. Hon. Lady has told us this afternoon.

Mrs. Margaret Thatcher: Are you calling me a liar, Mr. Kinnock? *[General uproar]*

Mr. Kinnock: Of course I am, you bossy old bag. *[Labour cries of 'Good on yer, Neil', 'Sock it to her', etc.]*

Mrs. Margaret Thatcher: If you were a gentleman you would take back that insolent remark.

Mr. Kinnock: If you weren't a barefaced, unashamed and totally barefaced liar, I might.

Mrs. Thatcher: O-o-o-o-o-o-h. *[Pandemonium, waving of order papers, scuffles break out]*

Mr. Kinnock: Liar, liar,
       Pants on fire! *[Low yield nuclear explosion takes place on Labour benches]*

Mr. Tam O'Looney (Binns. Lab.): Could I just bring up the subject of the General Belgrano . . . . . *[House empties]*

To be continued

BABY COTTON

"What I like", Baby Cotton told me, "is somewhere warm and private". And there's no doubt that this lovely womb suits her to a tee. She moved in 9 months ago and told me "I knew at once it was me and I did virtually nothing to it."

Baby Cotton has simple tastes and her only complaint about the small single womb was that the rent was rather high at £6,500. However, she did confess to me later, that "Daddy paid up and he's frightfully well off."

When I met Baby Cotton she had just left, having come to the end of her lease. "You can't stay in one place for ever" she said, with a wry smile, sucking her Farley's rusk and *(cont. page 94)*

Your ILEA books tonight

■ *The following books have been approved for distribution to all schools in the London are by the Inner London Education Authority Revised Reading Programme (Chair: Dame Ottoline Morrell).*

1. ROBINSON CRUISER: a contemporary re-telling of the well-loved but racist children's classic, in which the hero, a London gay, seeks refuge from police oppression on a desert island. Here he meets up with a coloured gay, Person Friday, and they proceed to establish a touching multi-ethnic relationship on all levels in their tropical squat.

2. LITTLE RED RIDING KEN: one day little Ken sets off through the nuclear-free forest where he meets the terrifying figure of Mrs Thatcher disguised as a wolf. Imagine her horror when she gobbles him up. *(Shurley shome mishtake? RK)*

3. JILL AND THE BEANSTALK: a contemporary re-telling of the well-loved but sexist children's classic, in which the heroine, a liberated young woman, sets off up the beanstalk to do battle with the Giant of Male Chauvinism. Thanks to her karate lessons at the GLC Women's Self-Defence Workshop, she is soon able to totally defeat the Giant and returns home to live happily every after with her live-in friend Ms Muppett.

4. TOM BROWN'S SCHOOLDAYS: Tom Brown is delighted when, instead of being sent off to the all-male elitist bastion of privilege, i.e. Rugby School, he is instead lucky enough to go to Tulse Hill Comprehensive, where he can mix in the multi-ethnic, poly-sexual learning environment and read the above books.

THAT NAZI PRINCESS AN APOLOGY

IN THE light of certain documents which have now come into our possession, we now recognise that Baron von Heineken, the father of the much-loved and popular Princess Michael of Kent, was not, as some have suggested, a hardened, veteren Nazi war criminal, but was in fact one of Hitler's most deadly enemies inside Germany, working for allied intelligence throughout the war.

The Baron, a genial, twinkling eyes, lovable old gentleman, was enormously popular among the tenants on his Westphalian lager farm, where he bred partridges and invented the famous beverage which has made his name famous across the world.

When the war came, the Baron was personally asked by his old friend Winston Churchill to remain in Germany as an undercover member of the SS in order to organise relief work among the victims of Nazi persecution.

WAR HERO

The Baron was so courageous at his undercover work that when the war was over he decided to retire to Paraguay to escape the recriminations of his fellow-Germans who felt he had "let down his country" by his heroic work for the allied cause.

BOTTLE BANK

Aunli

LONDON'S THIRD AIRPORT TO BE IN OXFORD

Government's Shock Announcement

by Our Political Correspondent
A.N. Watneys

IN A surprise announcement from 10 Downing Street last night, the Prime Minister let it be known that the controversial third London airport is not, as many supposed, to be at Stansted in Essex, but is now to be sited in the university town of Oxford.

The shock decision, which has apparently been made only in the last week, is likely to provoke considerable opposition from conservationists, since it appears that a number of buildings of historic interest would have to be demolished to accommodate the new airport.

DC-10 DOWNING STREET

Last night government sources were strenuously denying that the airport decision had been made on the direct personal orders of Mrs Thatcher, although it was admitted that in recent days the Prime Minister has been showing a keen interest in a number of environmental issues related to "the South Midlands area in general and the city of Oxford in particular".

It has, for instance, been suggested since last Tuesday that the new M-40 motorway should be re-routed away from the prized north Oxfordshire countryside to a new line running through Oxford's High Street to All Souls College, which is to be modernised as a Trust House Forte service area.

MRS T-JUNCTION

It is believed in government circles that the new motorway will facilitate the government's new plan (as of last Tuesday) to use Christ Church Meadow as the main dumping ground for nuclear waste.

Further plans drawn up since Tuesday are believed to including the placing of a Cruise Missile base on the site of the former Magdalen College, and the choice as a nuclear underground testing zone of the Sheldonian Theatre.

ON OTHER PAGES

Why I Couldn't Care Less About Not Getting An Honorary Degree – by Mrs Thatcher. (Exclusive)

"Yes, death's been good to me"

Mr. Scargill's Historic Speech

*A CUT OUT 'N' KEEP SOUVENIR TO MARK THE
END OF THE MINERS' STRIKE*

Mr Scargill about to address his loyal followers from behind a 300 man police escort.

What we are witnessing today is a total victory for this union. This is the most historic moment in the history of this world or any other, and its members. When the government and the Coal Board claim that 100% of the miners have returned to work, they have not taken into account the millions of miners who have not yet been born who will show a total commitment to the principles that we have fought and died for in this historic struggle, this resistance movement against the horrors of Nazi Germany and the ruthless policies of genocide practised by the Thatcher government which make anything going on in Ethiopia look like a tea-party. What this historic strike has

shown, beyond all doubt, is that the working class is not prepared to lie down and be trampled on by people like MacGregor and Thatcher in the way that we have just have been. This costly and damaging dispute, which has already cost this country £ [fill in any huge figure that comes into head] . . . no preconditions . . . fighting for jobs, communities and pits . . . we do not accept the Coal Board's figures . . . these magnificent men in their flying machines . . . (raves on in this vein for several hours). . .

And finally I would just like to say this. That when the history of this historic strike is written, it will show conclusively that all the blame for this great and glorious

victory must be placed firmly at the door of those cowards and scabs in the Labour movement who failed to support me in my attempt to carry out the wishes of my membership as I understand them to be on the evidence of not carrying out a national ballot last April. I point the finger at such notorious traitors to the working class movement as Neil Kinnock, Norman Willis, Bill Sirs, the Nottinghamshire miners, the Derbyshire miners, the Scottish miners, the Yorkshire miners and all the other miners who failed to support me in carrying out my wishes. God rot the lot of them. Goodbye cruel world.